AF472362

A Man of the Prairie

ONE MAN'S LEGACY

By William Furman

authorHOUSE®

AuthorHouse™
1663 Liberty Drive
Bloomington, IN 47403
www.authorhouse.com
Phone: 1 (800) 839-8640

Published by AuthorHouse 02/16/2017

ISBN: 978-1-4670-2419-8 (sc)
ISBN: 978-1-4670-2418-1 (hc)
ISBN: 978-1-4670-2417-4 (e)

Library of Congress Control Number: 2011915916

Print information available on the last page.

This book is printed on acid-free paper.

ACKNOWLEDGEMENTS

Thanks to the contributors of information
that made this book possible.

Kathleen Cushing
Larry DeWitt

A special thank you to the
Sheridan County Journal Star
For opening their archives.

Thanks to Barbara Nighbert for assisting
in the preparation of this book.

CHAPTER 1

God is in heaven and you are on the earth

The birth of Evan Justin Furman was not a normal birth. In fact, Evan almost didn't make it into this world in 1887. His birth is just one of the things that marked him a little different than other men. He was born in a dugout on a homestead in northwestern Nebraska, 12 miles from any town.

Two years earlier his father, James, had filed a homestead claim south of Rushville, Nebraska on the Niobrara River. To provide a home, he dug back into a hillside. Then using the dirt he removed, he shaped rectangular blocks that were stacked on both sides of the hillside opening and across the front. Logs and dirt were used to make a roof. This became a home that settlers considered livable but crude.

When the time came for Evan to enter this world, James was excited. He was going to be a father for the second time. Their first child was a girl; this time, James hoped for a son. Evan's mother, Belle, on the other hand was in an uncomfortable labor. She was in terrible pain. The birth of their daughter had not gone like this.

Soon frustration over took James. He tried to calm Belle but didn't know what to say. He said the only thing he could think of; "It'll be alright Belle. I know you hurt right now but it will be over soon." Belle screamed again. James became more nervous. Drops of sweat ran down his face. His shirt was wet. He had assisted in the birth of calves and colts but never in a human birth. Their daughter's birth had taken place in Iowa and a doctor did the delivery. James wasn't even in the room.

Belle could only mutter, "Ooooh, you don't know how much it hurts." Then there was silence in the room until Belle said, "My pains are close together – (gasp) - I think it will be soon!"

James put water on to boil. He laid out towels and another sheet.

He sharpened a butcher knife and put it in the water on the stove. But most of all he paced around the room. He was so nervous his hands were shaking. Their three-year-old daughter, Edna, could not understand what was going on. She followed her father around asking, "What's wrong with Mommy?"

"Mommy is going to bring you a brother or sister, but it is very hard for her."

Belle cried out, "Oh Lord help me." James said, "Edna, you go in the other room and play with your doll." She did so, with many questions in her eyes.

Belle began crying because of the pain. She screamed again. James realized there was something wrong and he had no idea what to do. Belle needed help that he could not provide. He must get someone to help. How? Where? He did not want to leave their daughter alone. Nor could he take Belle anywhere. Belle was crying uncontrollably and beating her fists on the bed. He knew two lives were at stake. Dilemmas were a way of life to homesteaders in the Nebraska sand hills.

What choice did he have? He said to Belle, "I'm going to get Mrs. Preston. Don't worry; I will be back with help as quickly as I can." He went into the front room and picked Edna up. "Mommy needs help and I am going to get Mrs. Preston to come over. I want you to stay in the house and play. Do not go outside. You will hear Mommy yell, but she is all right. She just hurts. I will be back very soon with Mrs. Preston. Then everything will be alright."

Leaving Edna alone to play, he then ran to the barn. Putting a bridle on a horse and not bothering with a saddle, James jumped on the horse and kicked him in the ribs. He urged the horse to an unsafe run toward his closest neighbors, Sam and Ann Preston.

James began yelling before he reached their house, "Ann – Ann!"

She came out of the house, "Is the baby coming?"

"Yes, and Belle is in trouble! I don't know what to do! We need your help! Please, please come back with me! Hurry!"

"I'll leave now and do what I can."

James jumped to the ground; "Take my horse; sorry he's not saddled. But there's no time to spare."

He boosted Ann up on his horse and gave it a swat on its rump.

He stood praying, "Please God, let her be in time." He then searched for Sam to explain the situation and ask to borrow a horse so he could return home. Sam came out of the barn when he heard the voices. Without much conversation, James was on a horse and running toward their dugout.

Ann arrived, and she soon realized Belle's condition was beyond her knowledge. She wasn't sure what to do. To her thinking, Belle and the unborn baby seemed destined for the grave.

When James returned, Ann told him, "I cannot do anything for Belle. The baby will not come out. I don't think it is positioned right."

"Can you turn the baby?"

"I don't know how. Maybe it will straighten up by itself."

James was about to a panic stage and Ann began crying. "I am so sorry James".

James asked, "Isn't there something we can do?"

Help would come from an unexpected source. For as soon as James left Sam thought he should tell James' mother, Mary Pearl Furman. She lived on a claim that butted against both his claim and James' claim. "Mrs. Furman, you are going to be a Grandma. James came after my wife to help. He said Belle was in trouble."

There was a reason James had gone to the Preston's for help and not his own Mother. His mother was a cranky woman who had a personality clash with Belle. Their relationship soured shortly after she married James. Contact between Belle and James's mother had been very rare, and not exactly pleasant when it did occur.

Puffing on her clay pipe, Mary Pearl listened, then announced, "Is that so! I think I'll go see this baby." Even though the relationship between Mary Pearl and Belle was strained, she seemed to feel the need to be present at the birth. She left for James' place immediately.

As soon as Mary Pearl entered the dugout, she became aware of the trouble Belle was in. Mary Pearl had assisted a doctor in the east before she migrated west and had been present at difficult births. She immediately began giving out instructions. Ann was relieved and Belle was in no condition to object.

"James, you go outside and take your daughter with you. Ann, you hold Belle's shoulders down. Belle, what I am going to do will hurt. Scream all you want." Mary Pearl began pressing, pulling, and shoving while Belle cried and screamed. After what seemed like an eternity to Belle, Mary Pearl was able to position the baby for delivery and Evan began to emerge. Belle was exhausted, but relieved. The bed she was lying in was soaking wet. She had been in labor for some time. Mary Pearl cut the cord and swatted the baby's rear. Evan wailed.

Mary Pearl looked at her grandson and said to Ann, "I've seen him. Now you can clean him up." With that, Mary Pearl walked out, saying to James as she got into her buggy, "You have a son."

She had arrived in time to save both mother and child. But unfortunately the relationship between the two women did not change never improved.

James was thrilled and relieved. He ran back inside to share his happiness with his wife and daughter. With his emotions swelling inside of him, he held Evan in his arm, and kissed Belle. She was too weak to respond.

James picked up Edna in his other arm and said, "You have a brother! Just look at him!" Then he turned and thanked Ann for her help.

"I didn't do all that much. Your mother is the one to thank."

James said, "I will, first chance I get. Ann, could you stay a little longer just in case?"

Ann said, "I want to go home before dark but I'll stay until then."

Belle slept until the next morning. She was soon back doing her daily chores. A homestead life was demanding. She not only had two little ones to care for; she had washing, sewing, and cooking to do. Then there was a garden to care for, candles to make, an a million other things. She thought, "Thank goodness Evan sleeps most of the time."

About 18 months later, Mary Pearl would be involved in Belle and Evan's life again. When she fell and broke her leg, there was only one place Mary Pearl could go: she had to temporarily stay with James and Belle.

Mary Pearl had a pet ferret that she was worried about. She talked James into allowing her to keep it with her at their dugout. This did not set well with Belle, but she didn't say anything until a calamity occurred.

Evan was on the dirt floor just crawling about and entertaining himself when the ferret, for some reason, bit off the lobe of his left ear. Evan let out a wail. Belle turned from the table where she had been working and saw blood streaming down Evan's arm and body. She threw a pan full of green beans at the ferret, hoping to kill it.

Mary Pearl hobbled forward, grabbed up the ferret and yelled, "Stop! He didn't mean any harm!"

At the same time Belle picked up a crying Evan. She had had enough.

She glared at Mary Pearl and yelled back, "That animal could have eaten Evan alive! Ferrets are not pets and they certainly do not belong in a home. You get rid of it. I want it out of here right now!" The conversation between the two women got louder and unruly. Both children were crying. There would be no compromise.

James was not in the house at the time and learned of the situation that evening. By then, Mary Pearl and the ferret had already left and returned to her home.

Fortunately, Evan's hearing was not affected. But there was a noticeable difference in his two ears: only one ear had a lobe.

Besides Evan's unusual beginning in life and the loss of an earlobe, there were other things and events that shaped his character and thinking as he grew into manhood.

As Evan grew, one of his boyhood thrills was going to town. It was special being in town and seeing things in the stores. Most of all during these trips he was alone with his father. He could ask him many questions without testing James' patience since James had nothing to do but sit. On one occasion Evan asked the question. "Pa, I know Rushville is out there, but I can't see it. I know our home is behind us, but I can't see it either. All I see wherever I look is grass and it goes until it meets the sky. Why is that?"

"Well, son, people can only see so far then the ground begins to fall away and all that is left is the sky."

"I still don't understand."

James thought for a minute then said, "I guess it is because this world where we live is like a big ball. So if you were standing on that ball and looked out, the ground would curve down and away from you."

"So are you saying we live on a big ball?"

"Well, I guess you could say that. We live on the earth and it is shaped sort of like a ball."

"Where did the earth come from, Pa?"

"I am not sure I know myself, Evan. But I believe this world was created by God. Just how he did it, I can't explain."

"He must be big and powerful to make all this land. Did He make people and animals too?"

"The Bible says He did."

"Is that the book you and Ma read sometimes?"

"Yes, it is."

"Pa, where does God live?"

"I usually think of Him being up in heaven."

"Pa, if God up in heaven and looking down at us right now, I'll bet we just look like two small ants to Him."

James laughed. "Maybe so, but I think He feels we are more important than ants."

During these trips to town, Evan's questions to his father were endless. He wanted to know about everything. These trips were the beginning of his education. He learned about the world beyond Rushville. He learned the importance of keeping your word to others. This became a hallmark of his life. He learned about the value of family and he never forgot it. He also learned about raising cattle and horses. How clouds and winds could be a clue to weather changes. He learned that work was expected of him. His father would repeat the scripture, "If you don't work, you don't eat."

Evan was smaller than other children. His mother worried about his small size.

Due to his short height and size, working in the garden, feeding chickens, and helping his mother were his assigned chores. When he was about age 10, James said, "Evan, it's time you started doing some man's work." Belle tried to intervene, but Evan was more than ready to do things he felt were more appropriate. Like all boys, he wanted to feel he was capable of being in a man's environment. The testosterone was developing in Evan.

Evan said to his mother, "I am big enough to go hunting with Pa. Why he has even taught me how to shoot." He recalled the first time he held the rifle. His father told him, "Keep the butt up against your shoulder. Now reach out your left arm, just far enough to hold the gun steady. Look out to the end of the barrel and place whatever you are going to shoot at right on top of the gunsight. Put your finger on the trigger and squeeze - don't pull." Evan became a good marksman in time.

Belle realized there was nothing she could say to protect Evan. He would learn the ways of a man's world.

The first assigned task his father gave him was milking the cow twice a day. The family milk cow was a very placid animal which Evan managed easily. He would tie her to a post and give her some hay. He would sit next to her right hind leg and place the side of his face against her stomach. Then he would grab a tit in each hand with his thumbs inside of his fingers, and squeeze and pull.

The next chore was feeding and watering the horses. Moving them to water was a challenge for Evan. He was supposed to lead them to the river to drink. This required them to have a halter on. He was too short to get a halter, bridle, or collar over the horse's head. There was no way he would be able to harness for any work. Evan thought about how he might accomplish the assignment. It dawned on him to lead the horse beside a wagon and climb into the wagon. He could then put a halter or bridle on a horse.

His size limited him at harvest time or with field work. Instead, he contributed in other ways. Evan showed a attitude for working with and knowledge of horses at an early age. Horses seemed to respond to him. Soon he was driving horses that were pulling hay wagons or hay rakes.

As Evan went through childhood, brothers and sisters entered into the family. Some of them overtook Evan in height and size, but he did not seem to mind.

All the Furman children got along well with each other. After their chores were completed, they would play hide and seek or ride stick horses. In the winter if the weather was too cold and when the darkness came early, the games of I Spy and hide the thimble were played inside the house. Another favorite was to put a string through a button then swing it around. When the string was pulled tight, then released, then tight again, the button would move and make a humming sound. A contest would take place to see who could make the loudest sound.

If winter weather allowed, they would skate on the frozen river, and if snow was on the ground they would slide down a hill on a scoop shovel.

Regardless of summer or winter, whenever the children went outside, Belle would say, "Evan, you watch after Leo." Leo was the youngest boy in the family, and became Evan's responsibility. For the rest of his life Evan would feel he needed to protect Leo. The two formed a special bond.

Sometime in the late 1890's, when Evan was 12 and his other brother J.B. was 8, the relationship between them changed. J.B., as well as the children at school, would tease Evan about his size. Evan normally took it good-naturedly.

Then one spring day as school was dismissed, J.B. and Evan tried to go through the door at the same time. J.B., who was younger but taller than Evan, said to him, "You're in my way, you little runt." J.B. cleared the doorway, while Evan was pushed back inside. Evan didn't say a word; he just lowered his head and ran out the door and right at J.B. With one blow, he butted J.B. to the ground, then pounced on him and pounded him with his fists. It didn't take long for J.B. to quickly say, "Stop! I'm sorry." He never said anything about Evan's size again. They were equals now.

They remained the best of friends. They worked and played together. They still rode their stick horses and fought imaginary Indians. A favorite pastime was challenging each other to a game of mumbly peg whenever they could use their father's pocket knife. The two boys would set on the ground and begin with the knife point on their shoulders and their finger on the top of the knife. Then the knife was flicked off, with the hope that it would stick in the ground. Whoever was successful then repeated the exercise with the knife on his elbow; the knee was next and the foot was the last position.

When Evan completed the sixth grade, he stopped going to the country school that his parents had started. His days became filled with helping his father with chores. The same would be been true for J, B. The family thought if a person could read and write, plus know their numbers, that was enough; there was work to be done.

When Evan was 14, his mother sent him alone into town for flour, sugar, coffee and the mail. This assigned task was not new to Evan, but doing so alone was. As he drove the buggy away, Belle watched and could not see Evan's head over the seat back on the buggy. A tear came into her eye and she feared a difficult future for Evan. That evening she said to James, "When Evan drove the buggy to town today, I could not see his head above the seat back. I'm afraid he is going to be a midget."

"Now, Belle, we have been through this before. Evan will be all right. He has grown some in the last few years."

"No, he hasn't, James. Look how much shorter he is than J B. The clothes I make for him have not changed in size for two years."

"Maybe so Belle, but there is nothing we can do to make him taller."

"I know that but I can't help but worry about what kind of life he will have as a man. I'm afraid people will take advantage of him"

Then after Evan turned 16, he had a growth spurt. In fact, he grew about two feet in a ten-month period, reaching a height of over six feet. He grew tall so fast that it would be three years before his frame filled out.

Belle had to make new clothes for him every two to three months. She told James, "I have never seen anything like the way Evan is growing. First he didn't seem to grow at all and now I don't know when he will stop growing; he just shoots up overnight. I don't have time to do anything but make clothes for him."

Size would never be an issue again for Evan.

There are other stories that could be told about Evan and his family as he grew into his teens. There were blizzards, a prairie fire, dust storms and droughts, all teaching Evan to respect nature and to accept changing conditions when they occurred. He gained strength and determination living through challenging events.

After Evan reached his full height, he developed an attitude of independence. He continued being respectful of his parents; the thought of disobeying them never entered his mind. Still, he began thinking about doing things differently than what his father did. An independent streak was surfacing. He felt like he was a man and had the freedom to do whatever he chose. Family life was not needed; he could take care of himself.

He approached James and asked, "When can I go to town by myself?"

James was surprised. He knew this day would come, but didn't think it was time for it yet. "Son, you are still a little young to go off on your own. You need to wait a year or two."

Evan was disappointed. He would not push it just yet.

CHAPTER 2

I saw that wisdom is better than folly

In 1904 on a warm summer day, the town of Rushville held a celebration for the dedication of the new Court House building. The town had grown to the point that it had won out over rival Gordon in the selection of being the county seat.

There were tables set up in the streets for the selling of food and drinks. The town band was to play at 1 o'clock with a horse race to follow. The Furman family went into Rushville like all the other families in the area. There would be no work on this day. They arrived about 11 that morning and had a picnic lunch. After they had eaten, James told the older children, "If you want to go looking around on your own, OK, but be back here at the wagon by 5 o'clock. They were happy to hear they could move around on their own. Leo stayed with Belle and James. Evan was now 17. He and the older siblings went searching for friends.

The girls and J B went to hear the band, Evan located 2 friends and headed for the horse races. He soon lost track of time and did not make it back to the wagon at the agreed time to go home. At 5:30, his irate father left town without him. Belle was upset with James but said nothing.

Much too late, Evan ran back to where the wagon had been parked. At first he felt a sinking feeling. He stood staring down the road. Finally he returned to his friends. His attitude changed to feeling more blissful. One of his friends, who lived in town, invited Evan to spend the night at his house.

Morning brought Evan the problem of getting home. He walked from one end of town to the other, looking for someone he knew. On his second pass, he found a neighbor at the general store and rode in his wagon most of the way back to the Furman homestead. He walked the last 2 miles, cursing himself for his predicament.

When Evan reached home, he found his father in the barn. James' eyes drilled right through Evan. Evan said, "Dad, I know I did wrong. I just lost track of time and didn't realize it was after 5. I am really sorry."

His apology was not enough; James' temper flared. "You need to be taught to do what you are told!" He tried to whip Evan with a bridle he had in his hand. At the first swing, Evan grabbed the bridle and pulled it from his father's hand.

Evan said, "I told you I did wrong and you know I have always done what you told me to do. I can't go back and make it right, but you are not going to treat me like some animal. That's not right either! I am bigger than you are and can do as much as you." James began to calm down. The outcome was a realization by both that Evan was now an independent man.

James just said, "You need to apologize to your mother. She worried about you all night."

Evan replied, "I intend to right now."

A corner had been turned in Evan's life. He was a boy no longer. From now on he would exercise his freedom to come and go as he pleased. He still would live with his father and mother, as well as continuing to work for his father. James never paid Evan for any work He never had money to pay him; meals and a place to sleep were about it. He had given Evan a colt when he was 16. This was Evan's prized and only possession.

After Evan told his mother all that had taken place, he told her how sorry he was for worrying her. Belle realized a change had happened and that from now on Evan would not be her little boy. It was time she thought.

From time to time, Evan worked for neighbors, which provided some spending money. Working on his father's place always came first, but at every opportunity, Evan was building fence, putting up hay, or branding cattle for a neighbor.

There was an occasion when Evan was checking fences. As he rode across a blowout, he noticed a barbwire that needed to be reattached to the fencepost on the back side of the blowout. As he reached the edge of the blowout, next to the fence, he heard the unmistakable sound of a rattlesnake. He hated rattlesnakes. He wanted to kill it, but he did not have a gun or anything else to use.

At the first sound his horse turned and started to run, but Evan held him firm and calmed him. The horse did move back beyond the snake's striking distance. The snake uncoiled and slowly began to crawl away. Evan dismounted and held tightly to the saddle horn so the horse could not run away. Next he removed the bridle and used it as a whip. With it he beat the snake to death. He said aloud, though there was no one to hear, "That's one more critter that won't cause any harm." Without another thought, he put the bridle back on the horse and reattached the fence wire. It had been nothing special to him.

Whatever work was to be done, he always completed the assignments, then even went beyond what was required. But when he was finished and the opportunity presented itself, he would head for Rushville. He enjoyed dancing, and the lure of cards tempted him, which in turn introduced him to whiskey. He over-indulged only once. Evan saw the room spinning around. He staggered outside and fell to his knees. He was so sick, his insides hurt from vomiting. He said to himself, "why did I ever drink that stuff." He had learned a lesson and vowed he would never get drunk again. Later in time, he pushed his limit on a few occasions.

One of those over-indulging times took place in a saloon near the Pine Ridge Indian reservation. A week later he was back at the same saloon playing cards. There was a young Indian, who had drunk more than he could handle, causing trouble and dared anyone to fight him. Evan started to walk out. The Indian's eyes settled on Evan leaving. He moved next to Evan and said, "Why are you leaving? You don't want to be where there is some Indian? You think you are better than me, don't you? So try and prove it!"

Evan had no intention of fighting him, but the Indian drew back and swung a round house. Evan raised his left arm to stop the blow and punched the Indian with his right hand. The Indian stumbled backward and fell over a chair. He didn't get up. Evan looked around the room, where a conversational buzz began. There were as many Indians as white men in the room. Evan didn't know if the men were pleased with what had happened or if they felt Evan was a trouble maker. Even though he had had a few drinks, Evan thought leaving was the right thing to do. He walked straight out the door and mounted his horse. By the time he reached home he had completely gained control of himself.

The next morning James asked Evan, "Where were you yesterday?"

"I was up at White Clay.", answered Evan.

"What in the world were you doing up there?"

"I heard there was going to be a big poker game and even Doc Middleton might be there. So I went up to see what was going on."

"Doc Middleton! He's a horse thief and murderer. That kind will lead you into all kinds of trouble."

"Yea, I know. I just thought something exciting might happen and I wanted to be there to see it if it did."

"Evan you may be 19 years old but you will be 35 before you have any sense." Evan said nothing. After a pause James added, "Oh, come on; we have fence to fix."

Evan's work ethic had been instilled in him by his father. His beliefs of right and wrong could be attributed to his mother. (He soon realized that he not only had new freedoms, but that he was responsible for his actions.) Another lesson occurred later that summer.

Tom Green asked Evan if he might be able to help with haying. Most of the hay work had been completed on his father's place, so Evan agreed to help.

The next day Evan started helping on the Green place by driving the hay raking team. As the day came to a close, Tom asked Evan, "Can you help one more day? I would like to finish this cutting tomorrow." "I'm sure I can. Pa said he didn't need me for a few days." Evan left for the day.

The way home went through Rushville, and Evan felt an awful strong thirst. "My throat is so dry and a drink would sure taste good. It won't make that much difference in getting home." he told himself. Then he met three friends who wanted him to play a hand or two of cards. "No. I'm tired and I'm going to help Tom Green tomorrow."

"Come on, Evan. Three is not enough for a good poker game. You can quit whenever you want, just get us started."

"Alright, but don't expect me to play very long."

Evan won four straight hands and looked at the clock on the wall. "I need to go."

"You can't quit now. Give us a chance to win back our losses."

Evan responded, "One thing I've learned in life is: if you have a good horse, don't ride it to death."

"What does that mean?"

"It means if you are on a winning streak your luck will change if you keep pressing it. Look fellows, I'm sorry you have been losing but I'll give you a chance to win back your losses another time."

"Oh, come on, Evan, just one more hand. I'll buy you a drink."

After a pause Evan said, "Well alright just one more hand." He lost that hand and the one after that. The lesson was yet to be learned,

The next thing Evan realized, it was one o'clock in the morning. He said, "Maybe none of you have to work tomorrow, but I do. I quit."

"Yea, we should, too."

"Charley, can I stay at your house tonight. It's too late to go home now and I have to be back at the Green's tomorrow morning."

"Sure, we'll find some place for you to sleep."

Evan did sleep that night – and into the middle of the next morning. He jumped out of bed and without any breakfast, he saddled his horse and left Charley's place at a gallop. It was one o'clock in the afternoon when he got to the hay field. "I needed you this morning. Where have you been?" Tom asked in an irritated manner.

"To tell the truth, I played cards till late last night and didn't get up early enough," Evan answered.

"Well, I admire your honesty, but I need someone I can count on and it appears that you can't be counted on. (pause) I got Ike Jackson to help now. Come back Saturday and I'll pay you for yesterday. But don't look for me to ask you to work again."

Card playing and drinking was giving Evan a bad reputation. He decided it was time to change that perception.

Evan left, mumbling to himself, "How stupid of me to get talked into playing cards last night. I not only missed a chance to make some money, I lost some money playing cards. And on top of that, I may have damaged my chances to work for others. How stupid! How stupid!" He had learned a lesson.

It was late fall before Evan found any extra work, and that was because a neighbor was hard-pressed to get his cattle to the railroad yard. Evan made sure he did everything right. There would be no mistakes made this time. His reputation needed rebuilding.

As he was being paid, Evan was told, "Thanks for your help. If I need help with branding next spring, could you help?"

"I would be glad to help as long as it does not have to be done at the same time as my Pa does his branding." Evan hoped his lack of good judgment last summer would be forgotten.

Going to town was still something Evan liked. Going to dances on a weekend was better yet. Making it into town during the week was a rarity. But on Saturday night he headed to town in hopes of a dance going on. No more poker for him.

On one trip to town, Evan witnessed a man using a whip cruelly on a horse, tied to a post. Walking up to him, Evan said, "That's no way to treat a horse."

"It's my horse, and what I do is none of your business! I'm going to teach this horse who's master."

"You may be the owner, but you are not teaching that horse anything. You're just being cruel. I am telling you, don't hit him again."

The man did. Evan reached out and grabbed the whip out of the man's hand and with one punch, put him on the ground. "Mister, a horse responds to kindness and gentleness more than to a whip. I don't care if it is your horse, if I ever see you using this again on a horse, I'll use it on you." He threw the whip to the side and turned and walked away. The man got up rubbing his jaw.

As Evan walked on, he hoped there would be a dance that evening. After all that was the main reason for coming into town. But there was no dance that night and Evan left town disappointed.

Two months went by without any dances. Evan felt like a child that didn't get a present on his birthday. Not only did he miss the dances, he missed the female companionship that dances provided. He liked being with the girls at the dances. They were different than the ones he used to associate with.

One Saturday night, Evan sat in the town saloon sipping on a beer because there was nothing else to do. He could take it no longer.

He was thinking somebody should do something about the situation. As he sat across the table from his friend, Floyd, he said, "How do you think we could get a dance going?"

"I don't know, Evan. I guess it just takes someone to start it. Maybe you should start one."

"Well, I don't know if I am the one, but I'm tired of just sitting around every Saturday night."

"So do something. You're the one that wants to do the dancing."

"O.K., I will." Evan said; he paused then continued, "I'll see if we could use the opera hall. And I'll get the paper to write something about having a dance."

"Good luck on that."

The following Monday, Evan found an excuse to go to Rushville. His first wish was fulfilled. Yes, the opera hall could be used and there would be no charge if Evan would see to it that it was cleaned up afterwards. There was one other requirement – no drunks and no fights. Any trouble or damage would mean a sizable payment.

Next stop was the newspaper office. There, things didn't go so well. Evan asked, "Would you write an announcement about a dance to be held?"

"No, but if you pay for an advertisement about it, I'll print it." That wasn't what Evan wanted to hear.

"What if I write something myself. Would you put it in the paper?"

"Tell you what: if you write a letter to the editor, we'll print that at no charge. We always print letters to the editor. We have been doing that ever since the paper started."

Evan started thinking about what he was getting into. But then he thought, "Why not, and if I'm going to put this much effort into having a dance, I might as well try to have more than one dance."

Back he went to see Mr. Hoyt. "Would the Opera hall be available on more than one Saturday night?"

"Yes but not for free. Letting you use it once for nothing is one thing but using it repeatedly is different. You'll have to pay $10 for each Saturday night and if something else is already scheduled, you can't use it."

"I can't pay $10 for a dance. What if I do some work for you?"

"I don't have any work for you to do. Why don't you charge 50 cents or a dollar to everyone that shows up?" Evan wondered if people would be willing to pay something to dance.

Evan walked out muttering aloud, "First things first, the first dance hasn't taken place yet." People passing him on the street turned and looked at him. He smiled sheepishly. He still needed to have an announcement in the paper. After giving a great deal of thought to what he would say and making a couple of false starts, he wrote:

> *To the editor,*
>
> *A large number of the young people living in the Rushville area have expressed a desire to co-operate in the organization of a society, to be known as the "Country Club", for the purpose of holding a series of dances at "Hoyt's Opera Hall" during the winter months of 1908-1909. In order to facilitate a meeting of those interested and to complete the organization, it has been arranged to give an entirely free dance on the evening of November 13, 1908, beginning at 8:30 o'clock. Yourself, and more especially, your lady are invited to attend this first meeting of the "Country Club" and don't forget, please, how uninteresting it will be to you if your lady is not there. It is the intention in giving this dance, to invite all dancers living outside the village of Rushville. If you do not get a personal invitation it is because of lack of information in making up the list. You are invited to come and will be expected just the same.*
>
> *Very truly yours,*
> *Evan Furman*

Evan didn't know if young people wanted to form a society or not, he just thought it sounded good.

The Rushville newspaper did print the letter and the news about the dance spread throughout the county. Many young people expressed an interest in having a big dance, but how many would attend was questionable. Men began asking the young ladies to attend with them. Those who were turned down asked their sister or cousin.

Evan didn't have any one girl that held his interest; he just liked all girls. If he asked a girl to go to the dance with him, he knew he would be obligated to spend most of his time with her. That did not appeal to him. If he took his sister, Ava, he would be free to dance with different girls.

"Ava, would you go to the dance with me?"

"Evan, if I go with you, can I trust you to not get into trouble and to take me home after the dance is over?"

"I have no intention of drinking or causing a problem. This is going to be a very special affair. But I will warn you that I plan to dance with as many girls as I can."

"That's O.K.; I might meet some nice boys as well."

"I will take you home just after I make sure everything is cleaned up after the dance."

The night of the dance finally arrived. Evan and Ava got to the Opera Hall early. Evan was nervous about someone showing up to provide music. One fellow had told him he would play his fiddle if he was not doing anything else that night. He did show up, as well as the lady who played the piano at the Presbyterian Church. There were 20 couples that came to the dance and three single men. Evan kept an eye on them. He planned to stop any trouble before it started. The music started and soon most were dancing.

The first dance was a square dance number. Everyone knew how to square dance and it helped to get everyone feeling good. A few waltzes followed, but before long the music got livelier and two-step and turkey trot dances filled in for the rest of the evening.

Changing partners was easy to accomplish since several couples were brother and sister or some relative. After the third dance, Evan asked Milla Jackson to dance. Evan had noticed her when she came into the hall. She was wearing a green dress with lace around the neck, which seemed a contrast to her dark hair and eyes. She had a petite frame with an hourglass figure. Her hair was rolled in a pompadour style. Evan thought she was the prettiest girl in the room. Milla had come to the dance with her brother, Herbert.

Milla had noticed Evan as well. He was tall and well built. His face had the ruggedness of most prairie men, yet there was softness when he smiled. His brown hair and brown eyes completed his stoic demeanor.

Evan was pleased when she accepted his invitation to dance. "You're a gifted dancer, Milla."

"You're not bad yourself, Evan. And I must say I am impressed by the way you organized everything for this dance."

"Well, somebody needed to do something. Besides, all I did was talk to some people and write a letter."

"Maybe so, but not everyone could do it. You are a different fellow than what I thought you were."

"What do you mean? Or should I ask, what did you think I was?"

"I'm not sure. I had heard you drank a lot and played poker, which had gotten you into a fight a time or two."

"I won't deny doing some things that I regret, but that's not who I am."

"I hope not. You seem like a very gentle and thoughtful person."

The dance ended and Evan thanked Milla. Next he asked Sarah Snider to dance, and then Mary Johnson. He went back to Milla Jackson three times asking for a dance; twice he was successful. Evan thought there was something different about Milla from the other girls he knew.

After the last dance, Evan spoke to the group, "I hope everybody had a good time." There was a unanimous agreement. "We had a great time," someone said. Another said, "Thank you for making this dance possible."

Evan felt encouraged. He said, "If there was another dance, would you be willing to pay for the use of the hall, and pay something to those who provided the music?"

"It depends on how much money you are talking about."

Evan replied, "I don't know for sure. Maybe 50 cents; certainly no more than a dollar."

One man spoke up, "I think 50 cents for a couple would be fair." Several nodded their heads in agreement.

"Alright, let's try it. How about the first Saturday night in December, if the hall is available?" Evan asked.

Milla Jackson said, "That's fine if there is not a lot of snow."

Evan was pleased to hear her speak in support. "I'll make sure the hall is available. If it is, I'll ask the newspaper to announce it. You people need to tell your friends about it and be ready to help out." Evan knew that more people would be needed if the charge was only 50 cents per couple. He was taking a financial risk. He just felt certain things would work out.

CHAPTER 3

If two lie down together, they will keep warm

The next few days all Evan thought about was Milla Jackson. He decided she was about the prettiest girl he had ever seen. He couldn't wait for another dance, so he could be near her. But what if she didn't go? He thought she would, after all she talked in support about it.

Evan learned the Opera Hall would be available the first Saturday in December. After some conversation about when the $10 payment would be made, Mr. Hoyt agreed to accept payment after the dance. The newspaper posed a problem. They wanted Evan to pay for an advertisement about the dance. Instead, Evan proposed an alternative. "Tell you what, you and your wife come to the dance free, no charge. Not only will you have a good time, you can also give a first-hand report about it in the next paper you print."

"That doesn't sound like a good deal to me."

Evan tried a different approach, "Why don't you ask your wife if she would like to go to a dance? If she does, then bring her to the dance and there will be no charge. In exchange would you print an announcement about the dance?"

After giving it some thought, the newspaperman agreed. "But I'll be surprised if my wife would want to go. If she doesn't, then no free advertisement"

Three days later, there was an announcement about the dance in the Rushville newspaper. Evan felt good about the way everything fell into place for another dance. His thoughts now were, "If only the snow will stay away, or if there could be very little snow." It would be another 10 days before the second dance.

Evan began to wish he had an excuse to go over to the Jackson place. Finally he got up the nerve to go over and ask Milla to go to the dance with him. He was nervous about asking. He'd been around girls; he had sisters, and he had messed around with some of the women in saloons, but this was different. Milla was a proper lady. He rode very slowly toward the Jackson place and tried to think of the right words to say. When he got there, Milla had gone to town with her mother. Evan was relieved, but sorry. He visited with Milla's brothers for a while, then left.

When Milla and her mother returned, her brothers couldn't wait to talk to her. "You'll never guess who showed up while you were gone." Milla, thinking it was a neighbor, said, "Who?"

"Evan Furman."

"Evan Furman, what in the world did he want?"

"He said he wanted to see you. He sure didn't ride all the way over here to see us."

Milla asked, "What did he say?"

"He asked if you were here. When we told him no, he asked if you were going to the dance with anyone."

"What did you tell him?"

"Told him we didn't know if you were going or not." Milla just smiled and walked toward the house.

Two days later Evan returned, and this time Milla was there. He wanted to talk with her privately, but her brothers kept hanging around. Finally, Mr. Jackson happened by and assigned each boy a chore that would occupy their time for an hour or two.

After some talk about the weather and what grew best in the garden, Evan could wait no longer. He blurted out, "Milla, would you go to the dance with me next Saturday?"

"It's kind of you to ask me, Evan. I would like to go to the dance. Are you sure it's not out of your way to take me?"

Evan's courage seemed to grow. "Not at all. Just the thought of spending the evening with you would be priceless."

"Oh my, that is flattering. After a statement like that I can only say, I'll go with you."

When Evan was far enough away from the Jackson house, he let out a yell and broke the horse into a gallop.

On the day of the second dance, Evan borrowed his father's buggy and left in plenty of time to pick up Milla and get to town before the dance began. Evan and Milla danced every dance that night.

There would be no swapping of partners on this night. Conversation between the two flowed like a mountain stream in the springtime. Evan found himself more and more attracted to Milla Jackson.

They left the dance a little early because Evan felt Milla needed to be home by a reasonable hour; and he wanted to make a good impression on Milla's father. Besides, by the time he took her home and got to his house, it would probably be two o'clock in the morning. He was glad it was not branding time or haying time. His father never put up with late sleepers when there was work to be done.

Before Evan and Milla left, Evan asked Ed Green to take the money that had been collected and to close up the hall after the dance was over. Evan promised to come by the next day to pick up the money.

The winter was mild that year for Nebraska, and Evan was glad. On Sundays he would ride over to the Jackson place to see Milla. On New Year's Eve there was to be a third dance, and Evan and Milla planned to go. Milla was going to wear the green dress, which she had made, because Evan had commented that she looked so nice in it.

About 3:00 o'clock in the afternoon the last day in December, Evan started for the Jackson's in his father's buggy. Just before he left, James said, "Evan, it looks like a storm is moving in. I'm not sure it is very smart to start to the Jackson's." Evan had only one thing on his mind and he was not going to be denied seeing Milla. "Dad, it wouldn't dare snow on the day of a big dance. I'll be fine."

When he was halfway there, he saw a line of heavy dark clouds beginning to move in from the north and the wind speed was increasing. There was no doubt what was coming. Evan knew he was in trouble. He had heard stories about what happened to people caught in the open when a blizzard hit. He encouraged the horse into a run. It was closer to the Jackson's than it was back to his father's place.

The snow started slow enough, but the wind was still strong and Evan could feel it through his coat. As he turned onto the trail leading to the Jackson house, the storm's fury unleashed. Evan thought he could make it to the house, even though the snow was falling so fast and thick he could not see anything but a white blanket in front of his face. Drifts began to hide low places.

The horse began to slow to a very slow, precarious walk. The buggy was designed to go through deep snow and the snow was getting deeper. Evan got out of the buggy and began leading the horse. Soon he realized the buggy was too much of a drag so he unhitched the horse. He mounted and urged the horse on. Evan thought, it can't be much farther. Where is the fence that goes to their barn? If I can find it I can follow it to their barn. He had never been so cold before. "Maybe if I walk I'll warm up." He dismounted and reached his arm out hoping to find the fence.

Milla stood at the front window, watching the snow falling. She began to worry. Did Evan stay home or was he out there somewhere trying to reach her. She begged her brothers to go out and look for Evan.

"Milla, are you crazy? We would not get 20 feet away from the house before we would be overcome by this storm."

Milla turned to her father, "Pa, can't you do something?"

"There is nothing we can do without endangering ourselves, Milla."

Milla went back to the front window and peered out. The snow fall lessened momentarily. Then she saw something moving. "Father, Evan is out there! He's coming!" She grabbed her father's arm. "I saw him! Help him!" James Jackson looked out the window and confirmed what Milla saw. About 200 yards away from the house, Evan was leading his horse toward the Barn. "Boys, get your coats on and help Evan get that horse into the barn. And get him into the house; he must be about frozen."

Like all frontier people, the Jackson's tied a rope from the house to the barn during the winter. This allowed them to go back and forth without getting lost if there was a blizzard. Lyle Jackson followed the rope line to the barn to get the doors open. Carrying a lantern, Herb and Ike headed out to meet Evan. Herb said, "I'll see to your horse, Evan. You go with Ike to the house."

Evan was so cold and tired from struggling the last mile, he just whispered, "Thanks." Grabbing hold of Ike's shoulder, he let Ike lead him to the house.

Evan didn't realize how close he came to freezing to death until he was inside. His hands shook as he removed his coat. His feet felt numb and there was no feeling in his nose. Milla covered him with a blanket. "Oh, Evan, you could have died out there. You should have stayed home."

Evan answered between sips of coffee that Mrs. Jackson had given him. "There were only a few clouds in the sky when I left home. I didn't know I would get caught in a blizzard."

There would be no New Year's Eve dance that night. But Evan and Milla talked until one o'clock in the morning while the wind howled and the snow fell. They were in their own world and gave no thought to the storm outside. Evan decided that night that Milla was the woman he wanted to spend the rest of his life with.

After the rest of the family had retired for the night, Evan was still ready to talk all night but Milla was more realistic. "Evan we need to call it a night, it's after 1 o'clock. Mother said for you to sleep upstairs in the boy's room."

"I guess you are right. I didn't think about the time, I was enjoying your company so much."

"We can talk some more tomorrow because you won't be able to leave for a day or two."

Evan liked the thought of that. He had the urge to kiss Milla but thought he had better not. He simply said, "Goodnight."

Two days went by before Evan could think about leaving and going to his father's place. The snow had blown across the low places but the hilltops were mostly bare. Evan said, "I believe I could make it home if I stayed on high ground." Still, the Jackson's thought he should wait another day at least. Evan didn't need much convincing. Staying would mean he could be with Milla.

After another day, Evan left, but only after promising Milla he would go straight home and would be careful. Soon after leaving the house, he found the buggy almost buried by snow. He began clearing away what snow he could, and then he hitched the horse to the buggy. Pulling the harness and encouraging the horse, he was able to break the buggy free. The trip home gave him time to think about what he had to offer a wife.

Not much. He thought, "I own a horse, 15 cows that are breed able, and maybe $50 cash money. That's not enough for a man and wife to live on!" Then his thoughts wandered to, "Where could they live, and what would they have to start housekeeping?" He was frustrated. "How is a guy supposed to start married life?" The rest of the way home, he mulled over what he thought would be needed for married life compared to what he had.

Two days later, James and Evan were taking hay to the cattle when Evan asked, "Pa, what did you have when you and Ma got married?"

"You must be serious about the Jackson girl."

"Yes, I am."

James looked at him and stopped the horses pulling the hay sled. "Do you think you are ready to be responsible for a wife and a family?"

"Pa, I know the last two years I haven't done anything unless I thought it was enjoyable. But now, just being with Milla is all I am interested in."

"Are you sure it isn't just the thought of being in bed with her?"

"No, strange as it is, I think more about just being together like I see you and Ma."

James waited a few minutes, and then added. "If you have a wife, you can't be going to town to play cards and drinking."

"I know that."

"Well, maybe you have developed into a man. I wasn't sure you were going to for a while."

"I want to marry Milla, Pa, but I haven't got anything to start with or a place we could live. That's why I asked you, what you had when you and Ma got married."

"That was a long time ago, back in Iowa. I was teaching school and farming with my mother and brothers. I didn't have anything to start a home with, but I did have an income from school teaching. It wasn't much though."

"So how did you get a house and stuff?"

"It took a while. For three months we lived with your Ma's parents. The first winter, a neighbor let us live in a house he wasn't using in return for me building a barn for him. I got my brothers to help with the barn. They later helped me build a house for your Ma and me."

"So could we live with you and Ma for a while?"

"We wouldn't turn you out, but two families under one roof is not good. I have learned that in my life. You can have your bed and we could give you a couple of chairs and some other things to help you get started. We'll do whatever we can to help."

"Thanks Pa. Any help you can give is appreciated."

"When are you going to tell your Ma?"

"I haven't asked Milla yet. She might say no, but I hope not."

"When are you going to ask her?"

"Soon. I just haven't figured out what to say and figured out where we could live."

"Son, if you are willing to work at it, things have a way of working out. They don't just happen. It takes effort but it you can get through it."

"I'm going to see Milla this Sunday. If my nerve doesn't fail me, I'll ask her then. You and Ma will know it if she says yes."

"Good luck. I won't say anything to Ma. You can tell her."

Evan thought Sunday was a long way off, but it arrived all too soon. On Saturday he asked his mother to wash and iron his shirt, and he polished his boots.

Early Sunday morning, after making certain his appearance was at its best, he left in his father's buggy. All the way to the Jackson place Evan kept trying to put the words in order. He would say them one-way, then change his mind and say them another. Nothing seemed to sound just right.

Milla expected Evan and had made a picnic lunch. Her mother said to her, "What are you thinking? This is not summer. You and Evan can't go out and sit under a tree this time of year."

"I know it is cold, but I want to be alone with Evan. I don't want my brothers pestering us. We won't be gone very long and I'm taking two blankets to wrap around us. We'll be fine."

When Evan did arrive he visited with Milla's parents for a few minutes. He was anxious to be alone with Milla. He did not know how to proceed. Relief came when Milla suggested they go for a buggy ride.

They went toward the river, bundled in wool blankets. This was not the right time of year for a picnic. Food was not what was on their minds. There was not much snow on the ground and the sky was blue with the sun in full array. Two young people wanting to be alone would not notice the cold.

"Evan, you seem nervous. Is there something wrong?" Milla asked.

"No, nothing is wrong; just the opposite. I want to ask you something. I just am not sure how to ask."

Milla knew what was coming. With a smile she said, "My, you sound serious."

"Milla, don't tease me. I am serious."

For a few minutes, only the sound of the wind was heard. Then Evan stammered. "I want to marry you!" Neither said anything until Evan said, "That didn't come out like I planned to say it."

Milla put her arms around Evan, kissed him and said, "Yes, I will marry you."

"You will?"

"Yes, I will."

Evan rubbed his hands on his legs and let out a deep breath. "Asking that question is about the hardest thing I have ever had to do. Let's go tell your folks."

"Not just yet. Let's just spend this afternoon together." They stayed huddled together until the cold could no longer be tolerated.

Later, after telling Milla's parents, Evan left for his parent's home to tell his folks. It was after dark when he arrived. He unhitched the horse and went in the back door. His mother was still cleaning up from supper. "Would you like something to eat, Evan?"

"No thanks, Ma. Sit down a minute; I've got something to tell you."

"What is it, son?"

"I asked Milla to marry me, and she said yes."

"I'm not surprised. The last three months she has been the only thing on your mind."

"How do you know that, Ma? I never said anything."

'A mother can tell these things. Have you told your father?"

"I talked to him and said I might be asking Milla to marry me, but I haven't told him that I did it."

"He is in the living room. Better go tell him."

Evan went into the living room and his mother followed. After telling his father his good news, James congratulated Evan. "Where and when are you going to marry her?"

"She wants to get married in the Methodist Church. We were thinking about three weeks from Saturday. Milla said it would take her three weeks to make a wedding dress."

"Have you got a license yet?" James asked.

"A license? You've got to have a license to get married? Why do you need a license?"

"I haven't got a good answer, but it's a state law now. Seems the government wants a say in more and more things. So you will need to go to the courthouse and get a license before you can get married."

The next morning Evan had planned to go get Milla and then go to the courthouse for the license, but his plans got changed. James stopped him. "Evan, there are two cows stuck in the river. I need your help to get them out. I think one is about to calve."

"Can't J. B. and Leo help you?"

"No, they're both hunting for cows that have strayed."

Evan hurried to the house and changed into his work clothes. The license would have to wait. The next day the bull was missing and had to be found. There always seemed to be something that had to be done.

It was 10 days later before Evan and Milla got their license. From the courthouse they went to the Methodist Church to ask the preacher if he would marry them. He said he would and for them to bring two people to be witnesses. They were excited and wanted to spend each day together. However, Evan wanted to have some money to start their married life. He looked for work wherever he could find something that would provide some cash.

Two Saturdays later, Evan and Milla were married. Milla's brother, Herb Jackson and Clara Booth, a good friend to both were their witnesses. They spent their first night together in the hotel in Rushville. Milla's parents gave them a quarter section of land for a wedding present. James and Belle gave them four heifers.

There was no house on their new land, so they would live with Milla's parents until summer. Both Milla's and Evan's brothers said they would help build a house for them when summer came. They moved in late in August.

The house was a three-room soddie. It was a typical sod house. The floor was dirt and the walls were sod blocks of dirt that had been formed with straw and water. The front had two glass windows and a wooden door. There was one window on the side of the house where their bedroom would be. They did have enough money to buy tin for the roof.

They were young and happy and in love. They still went to the dances when they were held and to church services on Sunday mornings. Even though they had very little money, they felt secure. They had food to eat and a house to live in. Milla owned four dresses and Evan had a Sunday suit and two sets of work clothes. Money was not a necessity. They had good health and hope for a promising future. What more in the world could they need or want?

Evan worked for both his father and Milla's father that first year. In return they were given food, and some household items they needed to start married life. Evan was a strong man and willing to work at anything. Milla was a woman willing to help with the livestock, repair fence or plant a garden. Many times the two of them worked side by side. Having a good married life and being young allowed them to handle not having a good house and material things.

By February, Milla was pregnant and before November ended, James Floyd was born. He was named for both of his grandfathers; however, later in life, he preferred the name Jim. She now had a baby to care for, so Milla's outside involvement in helping Evan diminished. She did plant the garden the next summer and care for it. The garden would be the source of much of their food supply.

Evan worked for a neighbor now and then. Many times his payment was an animal, but he did gain enough money to make a down payment on 320 acres with a promise to pay the balance in five years. The total price agreed to was $800. He bred his cows the first year with his father-in-law's bull and he planted some corn, which did not produce very much.

The second year he bought his own bull and planted wheat, which did a little better than the corn. His cattle "herd" now totaled 24 cows, 20 calves, and one bull. Evan said to Milla, "We are going to be fine. In three years we will double the number of cows we own."

When the fall days grew shorter and the temperature was cooler,

Milla realized she was pregnant again. The following May, Milla gave birth to Jessie Isabel. The birth happened without any early telltale warnings. Evan performed as a midwife. Milla and Jessie handled the birth better than Evan. He accomplished everything that was necessary but when it was over he was wringing wet. He sat in a chair to recover. "Milla, birthing calves is easier than humans."

Milla, lying in the bed, reached out for him. "Evan, you did everything right. You should be proud of this beautiful little girl we brought into this world."

A smile was on Evan's face. "I'm very proud. No man could want a better family than we have. And I'm blessed with the best wife in the world."

CHAPTER 4

Death is the destiny of every man

In October of 1912, Evan's second daughter, Ruth, was born. Milla had her hands full with a three-year-old boy that was full of life, an 18-month-old daughter, and now another baby. Thinking back to when she grew up, Milla remembered seeing her mother care for her family. She began to wonder how her mother had managed to do everything. As a child she had never given any thought to parental troubles. Now she knew.

Milla still planted a garden and canned and dried the produce. She made soap and sewed clothes for her children. She carried in wood for the cooking stove and sometimes milked the cow when Evan was late getting to the house. All the work she was doing was taking a toll on Milla. She began to feel tired and at times dizzy, but did not say anything to Evan.

Evan kept busy trying to produce a crop that he could sell, caring for their cattle, and maintaining fences. He worked for anyone he could, doing whatever work was available. Many workdays were 12 to 13 hours long.

They had a mortgage to pay for the land he had bought and Evan wanted it paid as soon as possible. He did not like the thought of owing someone money. The entire time he grew up his family had been in debt and he remembered hearing conversations between his father and mother about their financial condition. His mother had worried about money more than his father, and sometimes there were raised voices when the subject was discussed.

By the spring of 1914, the mortgage was paid. They talked about building a real house of wood. "Next year we'll build a house with wood," Evan promised. By May of that year Milla was pregnant for the fourth time. She struggled to keep house and care for the three children. She did her usual canning that fall, but when winter came she was exhausted.

Evan could tell she needed rest. He spent as much time with the children as he could. He even tried to cook some. Milla was reluctant to let Evan cook. He would say, "lie down and rest Milla, I'll fix us something to eat." Finally she gave in but after one try it was obvious Evan's cooking efforts were not going to work.

"Evan, I know you are trying to help me and I thank you for your efforts. But maybe you had better leave the cooking to me."

Evan willingly agreed.

Snow came early that winter and stayed late. In late January of 1915 a blizzard hit the Nebraska plains. Evan struggled to keep cattle fed and watered. Milla was not doing well and Evan began to worry about her. Snow and wind seemed to be a daily occurrence which didn't help.

"Milla, I think you should go to town until the baby comes."

"Evan, I'll be fine. Besides, you can't take care of the children by yourself."

"We could all go to my parent's house in town. I know we can stay with them and they'll help with the children."

"We should not impose on them. Just give me two or three more days of rest. If I don't feel any better then, we'll talk about staying with your folks."

Two days later Milla did not improve. She seemed weaker and paler than when the other three were born. Evan was concerned. "Milla, you need to be close to a doctor. Just as soon as the snow lets up some, I'm taking you to Ma and Pa's house. We will stay with them till the baby comes." Milla did not feel like objecting.

Evan's parents had left their ranch and moved into Rushville a few years earlier. There was no doubt in Evan's mind that they could stay with his parents. And there Milla would be closer to medical help if she needed it. His mind was made up. But with the snow coming so often and being so deep, how in the world was he going to get his family into town?

To his surprise his father and his father's neighbor showed up about noon on a rare sunny day. James said, "Your mother is concerned about Milla and wants us to bring her back to our house in town."

"Pa, you don't how glad I am to see you. I have been trying to figure out how I could get Milla into town. Would you and Ma put up the kids and me as well?"

"Sure, we'll all leave the first thing in the morning."

The next morning James and his neighbor hitched horses to Evan's wagon while Evan wrapped up some clothes for the children and himself. Then he helped Milla dress with as much clothing as she comfortably could. As he wrapped Milla in two blankets he said to her, "We're taking you to town this morning. I will put you in Pa's buggy between him and me. I hope you will be warm enough in these blankets. Pa's neighbor will bring the kids in the wagon. There is a lot of snow to go through.

"I'll be alright. Just look after the children."

"I will." Then he said to the children, "Put on two layers of clothes and your coats. Get in the wagon and sit close together in the bed. We are going into Grandpa and Grandma's house for a few days."

As he carried Milla outside, she winced a little but said nothing. Evan kissed her and said, "I know you may not think this is necessary, but this is best for all of us. You'll be better off with help nearby when the baby comes."

Evan put Milla in James' buggy and tried to make her as comfortable as possible. He climbed in next to her and put his arm around her. James started back using the trail he had made in getting to Evan's house. James' neighbor and the children followed in the wagon. The children huddled together in the wagon bed just behind the seat. The cold did not seem to bother the men as much as it did the children. Fortunately it was not snowing.

The trip to town seemed to take forever. It did take more time than normally because of the drifts and deep snow. James tried to follow high ground rather than the road.

All the way to town Evan worried about Milla. Twice he asked her, "Milla, are you alright?" Each time a weak answer came, "I'm alright, just cold." Evan would rub her arms and back. His father said, "She'll be alright, Evan." It was late afternoon when they stopped in front of James' house. Evan got out, picked up Milla and carried her into the house. The kids crawled out of the wagon and ran inside.

James thanked his neighbor who said, "I'll help you take care of the horses and the buggy."

As soon as they were inside Evan asked, "Are you alright, Milla?"

Milla smiled weakly and said, "I am just tired and cold." The children gathered around Belle and asked, "Grandma, you got anything to eat? We are hungry."

Belle, Evan's mother said, "Take Milla upstairs, the first door on the left. The covers are turned down. I'll look in on her right after I get the children something to eat." Then she asked the children, "Would you like some beef stew and biscuits?"

"Do you have any cinnamon rolls Grandma?"

"No but I'll bake some tomorrow. The biscuits are still hot though and I've some choke cherry jelly to put on them."

Jessie said, "Ok, we can wait until tomorrow for the cinnamon rolls."

Evan carried Milla up the stairs and laid her in bed. She was shaking so hard that Evan laid beside her to help warm her up. The children were enjoying something hot to eat. It had been a long day for them. James came inside, grateful for his neighbor's help but cold and tired from the day's struggles. Belle put out more beef stew and biscuits for James, and then she took some hot tea up to Milla.

Milla thought the tea tasted better than any she had ever had. It warmed her from the inside and she began to feel better. She said, "Evan, you need to get something to eat. I'll be fine."

Belle said, "There is some coffee on the stove and if the children left anything, there should be some beef stew and biscuits on the table." Evan went back downstairs after his mother assured him she would stay with Milla. Evan got a cup of coffee and sat at the table. His father, still sitting at the table said, "It'll be alright Evan. Milla has already given birth to three young'uns without any trouble."

"I know, Pa. It's just that she seems so weak this time. I'm scared something is wrong."

"She'll get stronger. You need to get your mind on something else, Evan."

"I don't think I can."

"Well, if it doesn't snow anymore, I am going after your brother and his wife tomorrow. She is due to have her baby about the same time as Milla. Your Ma says she needs to be in town too. If you went with me, you would be a big help and it would give you something else to think about."

"I don't want to leave Milla, Pa. Can't you get your neighbor, Mr. Ryan, to go with you again?"

"Evan, I can't ask him twice to go out in this kind of conditions. He was worn out from the trip to your place. I don't think he is up to another trip to J.B.'s"

"I won't say yes and I won't say no, I'll talk to Milla about going. If she is better, then I'll go with you."

The sky was a clear blue the next morning and Milla had a good night's sleep. Evan rubbed Milla's cheek with the back of his hand and kissed her softly. "Pa wants me to go with him out to J.B.'s and bring his wife into town. I told him I didn't want to leave you."

"Go ahead, Evan. I'll be fine. The baby isn't going to come in the next day or two. Besides, there is nothing you can do here but sit in a chair. You know you don't do that very well."

"I don't know, Milla."

"Oh, go on. Your father can't make that trip alone."

So Evan agreed to help his father bring J.B. and his wife, Iva into town, but only after his mother assured him she would take good care of Milla.

They hitched one horse to the buggy and Evan saddled another horse. It was cold, but with the sun shining on them and a light wind, it did not seem bad for February. They rode out of town just before 8:00 o'clock in the morning.

There was too much snow on the ground to follow the road, so they went cross-country on high ground where the wind had blown the snow into low places. Occasionally they had to take down a barbwire fence and replace it after they moved past it. It was mid afternoon before they reached J.B.'s place.

He was as glad to see his father and brother as Evan had been when James arrived at his house. James said, "We've come to take your wife to our place."

J.B. replied, "Good, I feel better about Iva having a baby with a doctor nearby. We can be ready to go in half an hour."

James said, "Maybe we should wait until morning to go back."

Evan did not like the thought of being gone from Milla for another day, but he knew his father was right. "I think Pa is right, Jay."

Morning came with clouds rolling in, but no snow. With Iva in the buggy and Evan and J.B. on horses, they left. The two men went first making a path through the few places where snow had drifted during the night. The trip back to town took less time; however, even though Evan swore it took more time.

James and Belle's house became a circus with two expectant mothers, two anxious fathers, and three healthy young children. The two brothers fussed over their wives. Belle cooked and tended to the mothers. James tried to occupy the children. No one complained about anything. "Family takes care of family," James would say.

Milla went into labor on February 14, 1915. Evan went after the doctor. The doctor followed him back to James' house and went right to Milla. Evan paced the floor, while Jay and his father tried to calm him down. The doctor seemed to be in the bedroom a long time. When a baby cry was finally heard, Evan was relieved. James and J.B. offered him congratulations.

What he didn't know was that things had not gone well. He began to worry when the doctor did not come out right away and announce the birth. Half an hour went by and then an hour before the bedroom door opened. The doctor appeared in the doorway wearing a blood-soaked apron and a stern face. "Evan, you have a baby girl." There was a pause, and then the doctor continued, "I'm sorry, but your wife hemorrhaged and I could not stop the bleeding. I'm so sorry."

"What do you mean, you couldn't stop the bleeding? What are you saying?"

The doctor paused, then said, "I am sorry; your wife is dead."

Evan just stood still. He looked at the doctor with an open mouth. His face turned white. Finally he cried in a loud voice, "Noooo! That can't be!"

"Evan, I feel terrible about this but it is true."

Evan turned and ran out the door. The children, not understanding what had happened, began to cry. Belle tried to comfort them, and James put on his coat and grabbed Evan's coat before going out to look for Evan. J.B. appeared on the scene to investigate the noise. Belle explained things to J.B. The doctor gathered his things together, offered an apology and said, "I'll try to find your son and see if I can be of some help to him."

Evan had not gone far from the house. He was just sitting in the snow, oblivious to the cold, and crying. James put Evan's coat around him and sat down beside him. James just put his arm around Evan. There were no words that seemed appropriate. Evan could not express the grief that overwhelmed him. Both just sat in the snow.

The doctor came upon them and expressed his compassion as best he could. After he left, James said, "Evan, you feel lost right now, but your life and that of your children must go on. You have to think about them."

"How can I take care of them? I can't cook. I can't breast feed a baby. I can't look after kids and work to provide money. What do I do now?"

"Son, let's go back into the house and talk about what can be done."

"I'm not ready to do that. I'm not ready to do anything. I just want to be alone."

"Alright, just don't go for whiskey; you don't need that."

"I don't want that. I just don't want to face anyone right now."

"Come back to the house when you are ready. And keep your coat on; it won't help anything if you get sick." James returned home alone.

Evan got up and started to walk, to no place in particular. His thoughts began with the feeling that his soul had been ripped out of his body. The woman he loved, talked about the future with, and who cared for not only him but also their children, was gone. In their conversations they had never talked about death. That was for old people or very sick people; not for them. He cried out, "Why God?"

Now he was alone with four children to raise. How could anyone know how he felt? He knew whiskey was not the answer, but he didn't know what was the answer. Not only was his wife gone, he didn't know if he could raise four children alone. He walked and walked. The world seemed dark and lonely.

"Where's Evan?" Belle asked when James walked into the house.

"He'll be along shortly; he just needs to be alone for a while."

"James, you had better go after the undertaker. The children don't need to see their dead mother any more than necessary. It will be awhile before she can be buried, with the ground being frozen."

"I guess you're right. I'll go now before Evan comes back. Maybe we can get Milla's body out of the house before Evan returns."

James and the undertaker wrapped a sheet around Milla's body and carried it down to the hearse while Belle took the children to the kitchen for cinnamon rolls and milk. J.B. and his wife, Iva, stayed in the bedroom they were using. Iva was upset by Milla's death and J.B. was doing his best to console her. It was after dark when Evan walked in the house. The children ran to him. Little Jim asked, "Will we ever see Mommy again?"

Evan didn't know what to say; his chin quivered. He put his arms around Jim and Jessie. Finally he said, "Mommy has gone to heaven. She can't be with us anymore."

They both started to cry and when Ruth heard them cry, she started crying, too. Evan held the children tighter. Belle stood by with tears running down her cheeks.

Then another cry was heard. It came from the new life that had entered the world. Belle went to check on the newborn baby. One life had ended and another life had begun.

No one wanted to eat that night. The children didn't want to go to bed until Evan laid down with them. After they were asleep, he got up and went into the kitchen.

Belle asked, "Do you want some coffee, son?"

"I don't know; I guess. Ma, how do I take care of four kids?"

"Evan, they can stay here with your father and me. You can stay, too, when you don't need to be out at your place. Things will work out somehow."

"I used to talk to Milla about things. I won't be able to do that anymore."

"You can talk to me or your father any time you want."

"Thanks, Ma. I appreciate that."

"What are you going to name the baby, Evan?"

"I don't know. Milla had some names in mind but she said we

would talk about names after the baby was born. I guess I'll never know what the names were."

"You might think about naming the baby after her mother."

"That's a great idea, Ma. Her name will be Milla; Milla Mabel Furman." The thought of the new baby being named Milla raised Evan's spirits. Somehow his wife still seemed to be near.

Evan J & Milla M (Jackson)
Furman

CHAPTER 5

The end of a matter is better than its beginning

Two days later, Evan saddled one of his horses and left his parents' house to check on the animals at his place. He found no problems, which was a relief. He moved plenty of hay to the cows and the two horses he had yet to break. Most of the eggs that had been laid were frozen, so he destroyed them. He would check for eggs in the morning, and then go back to town.

The house was so quiet. Evan looked around the kitchen. Milla's apron was there on a chair back. Evan closed his eyes. He walked toward the bedroom, and then stopped at the door. He couldn't go into the room. He thought, "How can I come back here to live without Milla? I see her everywhere I look." He walked back to the table on which they ate their meals on and sat down. There was no thought of food; he was not hungry. He just cried.

Evan slept on the floor that night. There was no way he could get into their bed. He wrestled with his thoughts all night. What would life be like without Milla? Peace finally came to him when he began to think of the children. This was their home, too, and the only one they knew. "I must get over Milla's death; life goes on," he reminded himself. "I am responsible for four children. God, I need your help!"

The next morning, Evan made certain everything in the house was in order, and then he rode out to check on the animals. They looked to be all right so he returned to the house and prepared to go back to town. He found a few good eggs so he wrapped them in a dish towel. He would give them to his parents if he could get them back to town unbroken. He also put some dried meat and vegetables that Milla had canned into a feed sack. He felt the need to provide some of the food for his children. His parents should not have to provide all the food for his family; Evan felt that was his responsibility.

Until the snow melted, Evan alternated between his parents'

house and his own place. He never spent more than two days at one place or the other. The children stayed with his parents. They seemed to adjust better than Evan did to the loss of their mother. But the girls said quite often, "I miss my mother."

Two weeks after Milla's death, Evan's sister-in-law, Iva, also died in childbirth, leaving a daughter. Belle would have to fill the mother role again, now for five children. She dug down into the pioneer fortitude that she possessed in order to do what she must. Three men were in the house, but motherly requirements were not within their abilities. She was a strong woman and handled everything with no complaints.

With the coming of spring, Evan decided to take the three older children and move back to his place. This would give his mother some relief, which she needed. And he thought, there is just me now so I need to learn how to be both a father and mother. James and Belle tried to persuade him to change his mind, but to no avail. Evan stated, "I appreciate all you both have done but I need to look after our place and I can't do that living in town. The kids and I will work things out." On an early sunny morning they left.

It only took a few days before Evan realized he could not be both mother and father. There was too much outside work that needed to be done, which meant the children would be alone in the house. Jessie did what she could to cook and look after Jim and her sisters. Jim and Ruth objected to this arrangement. He tried taking them with him when he needed to repair a knocked down fence or find a lost cow. But that didn't work very well even though Jim would try to do what he could. Evan came to the realization that he either had to tend to the children or reset fence posts and chase cows. He could not do both tasks at the same time.

Evan could not cook proper meals and the children didn't like what he did cook. Jessie did a better job of cooking than he did. Nothing seemed to go right. The girls needed a female adult to talk to and do things he could not do. One night at supper Jim looked at Evan and said, "I miss Ma."

"I know son, I do too."

It became obvious to Evan, he must move the children into his folks' house or find a woman to cook and keep house, for his children's sake as well as for his own sanity. Trying to fulfill both roles was just not working. Keeping the kids at home was his first choice; the problem was finding a woman to help.

He began to ask in town if there might be a widow woman who would come out to his place to cook and care for the children. Each time a name was mentioned to him, Evan would seek out the lady. The result was always the same. None of the widow women were interested in living outside of town. Most of them had lived that life before and didn't want to repeat it.

One afternoon while in Rushville, Evan met a family from Hay Springs by the name of Van Buskirk. They had a niece living with them that had lost her parents. Her name was Mary. She was 18, friendly and outgoing. Evan liked her and he wondered if she would agree to be a housekeeper. He kept weighing the pros and cons of such an arrangement. Two days later, he decided to ask her to be his housekeeper.

The next day he left the children with Belle and drove his wagon to Hay Springs to find the Van Buskirk residence. They lived in town, so the search did not take long. He found their house and some information about the family. Her uncle worked in the hardware store and her aunt was always helping a neighbor or finding something to do at their church.

The sun was shining and the weather not too cold. When Evan stopped at the house, Mary was alone, sweeping snow off the walk. Evan re-introduced himself and asked if she remembered their prior meeting in Rushville. She did remember. This encouraged Evan to continue with some small talk. Then he asked Mary if she had given any thought about working some place.

She answered, "I have tried to find work in a store but no one seems to need help. I do some sewing for other people, but there isn't much of a need for that type of work either. In fact, there's not anything that a woman can do to support herself. I would like to have some income so I didn't have to depend on my aunt and uncle for my livelihood. Why are you asking?"

Evan asked, "Would you be interested in cooking and caring for my children?"

"Is your wife ill?"

"My wife died in childbirth four months ago and I can't handle everything that needs to be done. I'll pay a fair wage, and promise not to pry into your privacy."

Mary looked intently at Evan. "Not only do you surprise me with your question, I don't know you."

"I'm sure I did. And no, we don't know each other. But I need help in the worst way and you seem to be looking for a way to provide for yourself. I thought we might work something out that would benefit us both."

"My, but you are bold."

"I guess I am. Would you consider taking my offer?"

Mary thought for a while then said, "I am interested in some way to support myself. I can't stay here forever and expect my aunt and uncle to provide for me. But I'm not sure I would feel comfortable being in your home with you there and no other woman present."

"I promise I will not take advantage of you."

"Where do you live?"

"I live near Rushville, and I have four children that are in need of a woman's touch. Please consider accepting my offer. My children are good and they need someone to care for them. And I have not been able to find anyone."

Mary looked at Evan as if she was examining him for a job position; not the other way around. Evan had a face that was beginning to weather and a forehead that was white from being shaded by a hat. His eyes were soft and had a look of kindness. She turned, looked into the distance as if searching for an answer. After a long pause she asked, "Can I trust you to keep your word about not trying to take advantage of me?"

"I give you my word."

After another long pause, she said, "All right then, I'll do it. But if you do try to take advantage of me, I'll leave immediately."

Evan said, "You won't find that necessary. We'll go in the morning, if that is all right with you. That will give you a chance to talk with your aunt and uncle. I'll be back in the morning." Without waiting for a response he turned and left.

After supper Mary told of her encounter with Evan and of her decision. Mary's aunt and uncle did not approve of the arrangement.

Her uncle said, "Mary, if your father was alive and here I know he would tell you not to go with this man. You are young and don't realize what might happen to you. Stay with us. You will meet a man some day and get married."

"Uncle Tyler, I know this is not a normal thing but it feels like the right thing to do. This man seems trustworthy and I believe what he has said about not taking advantage of me. And my heart was touched when he said he had four children that needed a woman."

Mary did not say anything about her feelings that this was her only way to provide for herself. She didn't think they would understand her feelings of independence. The conversation went on into the night but they could not dissuade her.

Mary packed her clothes and what few personal things she had. She was ready when Evan stopped in front of the house with his wagon. Her aunt said, "Mary, I'll pray everything will be alright, but if there is any trouble, come back here. We will come and get you if need be."

"I will. You have been very good to me and I will always be thankful for what you have done for me."

There was an awkward exchange of pleasantries between Evan and Mary's aunt before he loaded Mary's things into the wagon. Mary and her aunt continued talking while Evan did the loading. Evan thought it best to keep at a distance. Again Mary was advised not to go. "I know you both feel I shouldn't go but I think it will turn out to be the right thing to do. Thank you for all you have done for me. I will write you when I am settled in."

On the way to Evan's house, they talked about their experiences in life as well as their likes and dislikes. They found they both liked many of the same things. Mary told how she had come to live with her aunt and uncle. Evan talked about his children and how they missed their mother. He told Mary the names of his children, their ages, and about their personalities. Mary felt her heart go out to Evan's children.

As they went on, Evan said, "Mary, I probably should have told you yesterday that my home is not as nice as your uncle's. It is a soddie. I guess I'm so used to it, I never thought about it."

Mary was surprised. She had not thought about the house she was going to be living in. It was too late now for it to make a difference. "That's alright; I won't mind."

Evan was relieved; he went on to explain that the children were at their grandparent's house at the moment. He would go after them right after Mary saw their home and got settled. As they approached his house, Evan thought the trip back home seemed shorter than it did going to Hay Springs. It was good to have a woman to talk to again.

He unloaded Mary's things and took them into the bedroom he and Milla had used. "This will be your room. I'll make a bed and sleep in the main room. The children all sleep in the room without a window." Evan added, "I was always going to put a window in their room, just never got it done."

Mary interrupted, "Well, maybe you can now."

Evan smiled and continued, "You look around and move anything you want. Fix things the way you want them to be. I want you to feel that this is your home as well as mine. I need to leave now if I am going to get the children and get back before dark. I hope you don't mind being alone for a little while."

Evan went into town for his children and left Mary to become familiar with her new surroundings. When he stopped in front of his parent's house, Jim ran out to meet him. "Hi, Pa."

"How are you and your sisters?"

"We're fine. Grandma is a real good cook, better than you."

Evan laughed and said, "Where are Grandma and Grandpa?"

"Grandma has gone to the store and Grandpa is inside the house."

Evan went in and was greeted by his daughters. He gave big hugs to all of them. His father asked, "Where you been?"

Evan said, "I got something to tell you; let's go into the kitchen." Evan continued, "Pa, I have hired a woman to cook and take care of the children."

James' eyebrows went up when he heard the news. "Who did you get?"

"Her name is Mary Van Buskirk. She lived in Hay Springs with her aunt and uncle."

"She must be young. I sure hope you know what you're doing."

"She is young Pa, but I don't have any other choices. The kids need a woman around them and someone to cook good meals for them. They will starve on my cooking. Besides, I can't take care of them and do everything that needs to be done."

"Do the children know about these plans?"

"No, I'll explain on the way home."

"So I suppose you expect me to tell your mother?"

"I guess so. I need to leave now if I am to get home before dark,"

"Well, sure as shootin', your mother will have something to say about this."

As the children entered the kitchen, Evan said, "We're going home. Everybody get their things and climb into the wagon."

They were ready to go in less than five minutes. Evan carried little Milla out and handed her up to Jessie. "Hold your sister on your lap until we get home."

Evan left and before the houses in town faded in the distance he said, "You kids are going to have a woman to cook and take care of you from now on. She is at our house now."

The children did not know what to say. They were quiet all the way home. Each one seemed to be thinking who is this woman? Is she going to be living in our house? They weren't sure what this was going to mean.

When they arrived home, Mary came out to greet them." "Hello, children. Your father has told me a great deal about you, and I'm looking forward to learning more."

Evan took Milla from Jessie while the rest slowly got out of the wagon. He asked, "Well, has the cat got everybody's tongue?"

Jim said, "No, Pa, we're just not sure what to say or to call this woman."

Mary smiled and said, "You can call me Mary or whatever you want to call me."

"Yes, ma'm."

"I know it will take some time for all of us to get to know one another. Right now I'll bet you're hungry. Why don't we all go in and have something to eat. I would like to hear what you have been doing at your grandparents' house."

Mary had fixed food she thought the children would like. She topped it off with an apple pie. When she brought the pan with the pie to the table, Jim was eyeing it as if he could consume the entire pie. Evan noticed and said to him, "Now Jim, you are supposed to take the piece of pie closest to you. But if that is not the biggest piece, then turn the pan around." Mary hid her smile while Jim turned the pan just slightly.

That night Mary read to the children just before bedtime. Evan listened from the kitchen table. Mary told them goodnight, then went to the cook stove and poured a cup of coffee.

"Evan, you have great children. I think we will get along just fine."

The arrangement did evolve into a compatible family but not without some problems along the way. Evan could go back to the chores that needed to be done and to finding work wherever and whenever he could. Mary looked after the children as if they were her own. Jim warmed up to Mary quicker than the girls. Ruth was next and finally Jessie accepted Mary into her life.

There was little she could do to improve the inside of the soddie. Mary thought, "What can you do with dirt walls? I can't even hang a picture. I'm just glad Evan put in a wooden floor."

Cooking had always been a joy to her and after Evan's cooking, both Evan and the children felt blessed by what was put on the table at mealtime.

A week later, after supper, Evan asked the children, "Well how did you like supper?"

"It was great Pa. Much better than what you cooked," Jim answered.

Mary spoke up, "Jim, I'm sure your father did the best he could."

Evan smiled and said, "It's true. I about starved the children with my cooking." Then he looked at the three children at the table and asked, "What do you think, should Mary stay?"

Mary was surprised by the question. Jim and Jessie answered together, "Oh my yes!"

Mary blushed. She now felt she belonged in the family.

Mary asked Evan, "What is your most favorite food that I can cook for you?"

Evan answered without any hesitation, "Cinnamon rolls. I can't think of anything better."

"Children, do you like cinnamon rolls as well as your father?"

There was a unified answer, "Yes, ma'am!"

"Then tomorrow morning we will have cinnamon rolls for breakfast."

Evan spent the days tending to the cattle and working with a young horse he was breaking. He was also building a hay sled.

One evening a week later, Evan and Mary walked outside after supper. "I'm glad you are here, Mary. Life is not as lonely and problems are not mountains any more. The children really like you and you have helped me to adjust from Milla's death. I can get on with life now."

"I'm please by your words, Evan. I too feel I have purpose in my life. I have become so close to your children in the short time I have been here."

Jim and Jessie had accepted Mary and Ruth seemed to be by her side most of the time. Both Evan and Mary seemed adjusted into their roles of father and housekeeper. Evan never approached Mary in a romantic way.

It hadn't taken very long for the news of Evan's "housekeeper" to spread throughout the region. Every time Evan or Mary went to town there were whispers about them. At first Evan chose to ignore them, but it was an uncomfortable situation, especially for Mary. The women in town seemed to be staring holes right through her.

Belle had heard enough; she had kept still long enough. "James, hitch up the buggy for me; I'm going out to Evan's place." James said, "Belle, there is some snow beginning to fall, do you want me to drive you?"

"No," she replied. "I'm going to stop all the gossip going on."

No more had she walked in the door to Evan's house, when she began, "Evan, you and Mary have a problem. Your neighbors and people in town are talking about the two of you living together and not being married. This arrangement cannot go on; if not for the two of you, for the sake of the children."

"Ma, we've done nothing wrong. We're not sleeping together, nor have I ever tried to force myself on Mary."

"That's true, Mrs. Furman," Mary shyly added.

"That may be so, but you are never going to get anybody to believe that! Evan, you are ruining this girls reputation. Mary either needs to go, or you two need to get married. It's as simple as that! Everyone for miles around are talking about the two or you!" Neither Evan nor Mary said a word; they just looked at one another. Belle left them and went outside where the children were playing.

After a long pause Evan said, "Mary, I just never thought about what other people might think. I am sorry if I have damaged your reputation. I guess you should go back to your aunt and uncle."

"Evan, I'm not sorry I came. I've become very fond of your children and I think very highly of you. But I haven't thought of you in a romantic way."

"Nor have I you. I do like you and have enjoyed having you here, Mary. You've been good for the kids and you've helped me through my grief for Milla. I don't want you to go."

"I'm glad you feel that way. I don't want to go. I want to stay here with you and the children."

"Are you saying you would marry me?"

"Yes, I will marry you, Evan."

"You've made me a very happy man, Mary. I'm sure the romance will take care of itself."

They went out and announced to Belle and the children that they were going to get married. Belle was satisfied and Jim asked, "Does that make Mary our Ma now?"

Evan said, "I guess it does, son."

"I'm glad. Now I've got a father and a mother."

After this Mary was always called mother.

Evan hitched two horses to the wagon and they all went back with Belle to town. Evan and Mary went to the courthouse to get a license and then to find a preacher to marry them. After that, Evan returned to his place while Mary would spend the night at Belle and James' home. Belle asked Mary, "Do you have a dress to get married in?"

"Not really. I do have a dress that I have worn for special occasions."

"I think Jay's wife, Iva, was about your size and I don't think Jay would mind if you wore her wedding dress. He brought all of her things here after she died. I'll look for it if you will wear it."

"I would feel honored to wear her dress if you think it would be alright."

"I'm sure it would be alright."

Evan returned the next morning dressed in his best clothes. When he saw Mary in Iva's white dress, he thought, "I am one lucky man to have had two pretty women in my life." They were married that afternoon. Belle and James were witness. They all returned to James' house. On the way Belle said to James, "I want you to go to the newspaper office and make sure there is an announcement of Evan' wedding."

Evan and Mary wanted to be alone so they walked. Evan was relieved that things were settled but he did not feel like a new husband. He simply said, "Mary, I'm sorry that we won't be able to go someplace and be by ourselves like most people do when they get married. But with four children and a barn that needs repairing, we just can't."

"That's alright, Evan. I didn't expect anything special. I'm just happy to be married and to have someone to share my life with. You – me – the children; we are a family and there is nothing better."

Some of Evan's family gathered at James and Belle's home that evening for a celebration. Evan, Mary and the children went home in the dark. Evan and Mary shared the same bed that night. Neither Evan nor Mary felt comfortable at first but after they touched one another, human desires took over.

The newspaper announced their marriage, so the next time they were in Rushville there were not as many whispers. But there was a few "it's about time" or maybe a "they did the right thing" that could be heard. Evan and Mary were accepted as a normal family.

Life became routine, except from time to time something out of the ordinary would occur. In those days, no one locked their house when they left home. It was considered inhospitable to do so. Occasionally a traveler would stop in the middle of the day to rest at whatever house he might be near. The custom was to offer food and drink to the traveler. If no one was at the home, the traveler was free to eat what he could find and then leave some money for payment.

While Evan and the entire family were in town one day, they had a traveler at their house. Before they left, Mary, as was her custom, had baked some bread containing the food scraps left in the dish washing pan. This would normally be fed to their dog. She left a loaf of this bread on the cook stove when they went to town. When they returned, there was 50 cents and a note saying, "This was the best bread I ever ate."

After reading the note Evan said, "Well the dogs never died so I guess this feller won't either."

CHAPTER 6

A good name is better than a fine perfume

The weather that winter was brutal and Evan lost half of his cattle. His attitude about farming and raising cattle changed. The risk in raising cattle was more than he was willing to endure. He started thinking about some other ways to provide for his family. He thought about the automobiles that were beginning to be seen.

Evan's father was talking about the automobile business and he was considering selling them in Rushville. Evan said to Mary, "Automobiles are going to be a thing of the future. Maybe I should get involved. It sounds more promising than farming."

Mary had struggled through the winter in a different way than Evan. Living in a three-room sod house with only three windows and a door had provided a drab environment day after day. The dirt walls seemed to close in on her. She felt the need of light and cleanliness. She longed for a true house.

When the weather began to improve, Mary told Evan how living in the soddie all winter had been about all she could stand. She asked, "Could we build a real house out of wood? I would like to have some walls that are not dirt and a house that I could clean."

"I didn't realize you felt that way, Mary. Telling me about how you feel just made up my mind about what I have been thinking."

"What do you mean, Evan?"

"Like I told you the other day I've been thinking about doing something besides farming. I want to try selling automobiles. With the cattle we lost and the wheat damaged by the hail last August, we have little money left. Farming is so uncertain. Maybe there is money to be made selling automobiles."

"I'm surprised to hear you say that Evan. I supposed you would always farm or raise cattle like your father."

"I want to try something different, something new."

"If you feel that way, then I say try it."

They decided to sell what they had and move into town and go into the automobile business. Since his father was starting to sell automobiles in Rushville, Evan thought Hay Springs might be where he could start in the automobile business.

From the sale of their cattle, tools, and farming implements Evan raised enough cash to lease a building in Hay Springs. The land was leased to a neighbor. The building was large enough to display an automobile and do repairs inside. The next step was completed when he successfully completed arrangements to start selling Reos.

He also found a house he could rent in Hay Springs. The house was made of wood and there were three bedrooms. Jim would have a bedroom and the girls would share a room. There was a large living room, which was separate from a large kitchen. Mary was thrilled with the house. She felt she had returned from the dark ages. Also she would also be closer to her aunt and uncle which pleased her. The family moved in early June.

The first morning in their new home Evan noticed a new attitude in Mary. He said to her, "I never knew until now how much you gave up when you married me. I'm glad that time is over and I promise you we will never go back to a soddie on the prairie."

Mary said to Evan, "I am not sorry I married you what I gave up was worth it. But I am happy to be back in town and in a house made of wood." She continued, "One more thing I would really like. I want to plant a garden. Could you find someone to plow up some of the back yard?"

"I'll see if I can find someone. It may be a little late to start a garden."

"I know, but vegetables from the garden are so good, besides, a garden will save us money. We should be able to raise some potatoes and vegetables. Then I will can some for the winter months."

The family settled into town living and Evan proved to be a good businessman. He had an outgoing personality that made him a natural born salesman. After a slow start, he had success in selling automobiles. There was a great deal of interest in this new form of transportation. Evan was able to ride the wave of change in culture as well as transportation. Some potential buyers thought the price was too high and some thought the Reo wasn't the right vehicle but they all liked talking with Evan.

Within a few months Evan sensed he needed to have a second option for people to buy. He also wondered if being tied to one company was safe. He thought, "What if the Reo Company goes out of business? Besides if folks don't like the Reo, they might buy some other automobile."

He decided to sell Buicks if he could get an agreement to do so. His timing was right again. He contacted General Motors, a growing company. They were looking for dealers, so a contract was signed. Neither side addressed the risk issued involved due to Evan's weak financial condition. The Reo automobiles were discontinued a few years later. At that point, Evan contracted to sell Chevrolets.

The interest and desire to own an automobile was on the mind of most people. They would come into the garage to look at the new automobiles and begin a conversation about them

Being the salesman he was, Evan would tell people, "An automobile will take you farther and quicker than a horse and buggy. It won't be long before there will be no more horses being used to go places." Another sales pitch was, "There are 4,500 miles of graveled roads in Nebraska now and there will be graveled roads all over the state before long. Why, there are even some paved roads around Omaha and Lincoln."

His sales pitches were successful. He was ordering new vehicles monthly. He also sold the oil and gas that was needed. Soon he had an income far greater than he ever dreamed. He became wealthy and was highly respected in a short period of time. Mary was so happy with the home the family was living in. Evan persuaded the owner to sell the house. At the same time he bought a bigger building for his dealership in the center of town, and he also purchased the building he had been renting. So now he owned two buildings: One would allow for expansion of his dealership and for the other, he planned to rent.

Mary questioned the cost of owning a house and Evan's building purchase. Evan explained, "Mary we have no financial problems. Everything has turned out better than I ever hope for."

True the family had no financial problems. Whatever the economy had to offer, the Furman's acquired it. They bought furniture, new clothes or whatever they wanted. Evan felt he was on top of a mountain.

In 1917 the United States became involved in the war in Europe. All men between 18 and 35 were to report to a local draft board. Evan wondered if he would be drafted into the army. Mary did more than wonder; she worried.

On the appointed day, Evan, along with his brothers, reported to the draft board. Evan was excused because of his four children, much to his relief. His youngest brother, Leo, was also excused because of health issues, but his other brother J.B. was drafted into the navy. He would serve until after the war ended on November 11, 1918.

Evan sold his land holdings near Rushville and invested the money in expanding his automobile business a second time.

Before the war ended, the state government enacted laws for the establishment of hard-surfaced roads where there was heavy use. Evan used this to his advantage by telling people, "All these road improvements show the growing use of automobiles. It is so easy to go places now. Why before long, automobiles will become a necessity." He had made a wise decision to sell automobiles.

That summer a son was born to Mary and Evan. He was named Clifford Lee, but later he would use the nickname, Dub. The doctor who delivered the baby was paid cash for his services. The doctor was surprised but pleased. Not many people paid him cash.

The financial blessings continued. There was always a nice automobile parked in front of the house. They replaced the new furniture and curtains for their home just because they were tired of them. Mary could purchase store-bought clothes for the children and herself whenever she wished. She even ordered things from Chicago and St. Louis. The Furman's would be one of the first families to have electricity in their home and later, when it became available, a telephone. They were considered one of the prominent families in the area.

In 1919, Evan was in consideration to be a delegate to the constitutional convention; which he thought was a waste of taxpayer money. He was not interested in being selected and when his opinions became known, the people promoting him sought another candidate. Evan was relieved.

After it was over the following year, Sam Johnson, a customer, asked Even, "What do you think about the changes that were made in the convention? Are you sorry you were not a part of it?"

Normally, Evan did not discuss politics because of the possibility of offending a potential customer. This time he replied, "I'm glad that I wasn't selected because I didn't want to get involved in petty politics and I couldn't afford to be gone all that time. Still, I think some of the things that were approved are an improvement. I'm certainly in favor of the new amendment that limits salary increases for officials to once in eight years. That should give us some protection from tax increases."

"What about just having a one house legislature?"

"Sam, I already said more than I normally do. Can we talk about something else? Tell me, how is your car performing?"

Mary was disturbed because she didn't get a garden planted that year. Evan told her, "Don't concern yourself about not having a garden. We don't need a garden; we can buy all the food we want. You don't need to plant a garden ever again."

"Oh, but Evan, I like having a garden. Fresh vegetables from a garden are always better than what you can buy in the store."

"Well, whether we have a garden or not is up to you. Just remember it is not necessary."

While business was going well for Evan, his father, James, who had been selling Reos in Rushville, was having trouble. James was not the salesman Evan was and had not become as successful. When a drop in the market price of farm crops occurred because of a recession, farmers stopped buying luxury items like automobiles. Instead they borrowed to buy farming equipment. With the additional equipment, they started cultivating more land to increase crop yields in hopes of maintaining their income. It became a vicious circle. In time, this would create a negative impact on the land because of the loss of grasslands.

While Evan had trouble convincing people to buy an automobile or truck, he still had limited success. His father, James was not having any success. Then early one morning James' partner suddenly left town with the business's cash. James had to sell out and lost the Rushville dealership. Evan purchased James' unsold automobiles.

He asked his father, "What are your plans now?"

"I don't really know. I do know I am through with selling anything. I sure got left holding the bag. Thank you for buying the four automobiles I had. That cash and what I could get for selling the building covered most of my debts."

"So are you all right money-wise?"

"No, I'm broke. But your Ma and I will be fine because we still have the ranch with your brothers. That will provide all the income we will need."

After James said he was through with selling, Evan decided he would try to sell automobiles in Rushville as well as Hay Springs. He reopened James' dealership. Now he had two dealerships; one with a mortgage.

Evan said to Mary, "I don't like mortgages but this one should not last long. There is still good sales potential in Rushville. The business should produce enough to pay the mortgage off in five or six years."

"Evan, you have been successful here in Hay Springs. I just hope you are not taking on too much."

"I don't think so. I'm just taking a small chance which could develop into a good profit."

Evan continued riding the wave of success. Owning an automobile was no longer considered a luxury. Automobiles made travel from town to town an easy task. Farmers and ranchers found they were no longer so isolated. This in turn created a demand for better roads.

In 1921 the state responded by matching federal funds with state money for road improvement. The road going through Chadron, Gordon, Valentine, and all the way to Sioux City was designated as a major road. The Nebraska highway department planned improvements. It was graded and graveled. Evan saw this as a major selling point.

When he heard the owner of the Chevrolet dealership in Gordon was interested in selling out, he jumped at the chance to buy it. In order to raise cash to buy the Gordon garage, Evan sold the rental building he owned in Hay Springs. The buyer was Dan Blankenbiller, a pharmacist, who wanted to establish a drug store.

In August of 1923, Evan bought the dealership and announced the opening of the Furman Garage in Gordon, Nebraska with an advertisement in the Gordon newspaper, Gordon Journal. Not only would he sell Buicks, he would also sell Chevrolets. This would make the Gordon dealership the largest of the three dealerships. It also made Evan the largest dealer of automobiles in northwest Nebraska. The only downside was, it made sense to move the family to Gordon. Evan was not sure how the family would react to such a move.

That fall, Evan and Mary purchased a house in Gordon much larger than the one in Hay Springs. Mary was so excited about their new house. They moved, much to the disappointment of their children. The children said, "We don't know anybody in Gordon and we have friends here. We don't want to move!"

Trying to convince them that they would find new friends and that they would like their new home was not easy. After the move, the children soon made new friends and quickly adjusted to their new surroundings. Since each one had their own bedroom, they felt like special people.

Mary arranged to have some of the rooms repainted and convinced Evan to have the back porch screened in. She had new curtains made for all the windows. She was so pleased with their house, she said to Evan, "This is the best house that I have ever lived in. I feel like a queen in a palace." She invited the neighbor ladies in for tea. It was not long before she had made friends with most of the town folks.

Ruth was slower than the rest of the children in making the adjustment. She had freckles and felt that they made her look freakish. She complained about them often. Jim was tired of hearing her complain, so he suggested to her, "Ruth, if you want to get rid of your freckles, you need to find a fresh cow patty and rub it all over your face."

"That sounds terrible Jim. I don't believe it."

"It's true. If you don't believe me, try it. You'll see. Just remember you have to leave it on your face for 24 hours."

That evening when Ruth went into the house Mary looked at her and said, "Ruth, what on earth have you got on your face? It even smells!"

"It's cow manure. To get rid of my freckles."

"Who told you that cow manure would get rid of freckles?"

"Jim told me."

"You poor child, you have been the brunt of a bad joke. Cow manure will not remove freckles. Now go wash your face and clean yourself up."

When Evan came home, he told Jim, "You are a big disappointment. Your sister looks up to you and you took advantage of her belief in you. You hurt her very much. Now go apologize to her. Never take advantage of someone who trusts you."

"I'm sorry Pa."

"Go tell Ruth that you are sorry."

"I have."

"Don't expect any privileges or favors for the next month."

Gordon was larger and more vibrant than Hay Springs. There were more stores, which meant more choices when buying things. Mary and the girls would go to the beauty shop to get a "perm", as they called it. For entertainment, there were boxing matches held three or four times a year. There were more dances, a bigger movie theater, and a drug store that had a soda fountain. The young people found this the place to be. Evan and his family were enjoying their affluence.

In 1925 the state legislature passed a law taxing gasoline two cents per gallon. Evan was asked by a man opposed to the tax, "Why should I be required to pay more for gas? This tax is unreasonable!"

Evan answered, "I don't like higher taxes any more than you but we need better roads and more roads. There are more and more automobiles and people are traveling more. Who should build these roads and how should they be paid for? Gordon doesn't have the money to do it and the county doesn't either. That only leaves the federal government or the state to do it. And personally, I trust the state more than the federal government. But the state has to have the money to take care of roads."

"I didn't mean to start an argument. I just don't like more taxes. But what you are saying about roads is true."

"No argument intended. I just don't see any other way to do what needs to be done. Building roads is a big task. Normally, I don't believe in asking the government to do what we can do for ourselves. Road building is one thing we can't do."

Evan spent a lot of time driving from Gordon to Rushville to Hay Springs, then back to Gordon. The days were long for him, but he knew this was the price for success. The automobile business consumed most of his time.

Word of mouth comments were advertising enough for Evan's business. But newspaper ads for the Furman garage appeared from time to time. Usually these ads announced the cost of used cars and the price of a new Chevrolet. In 1926, a new touring car could be purchased for $615 or $640, depending on the type of tires that were wanted. The options were balloon or cord tires. A new sedan was $890 and a coupe was $790. There was also a roadster model, which was what Jim got to drive at age 15. His was red, which he kept until he graduated from high school. When Jessie turned 16, she got a new coupe to drive.

Having dealerships in three different towns provided Evan the opportunity to know many people in Sheridan County. Most people knew him as "E.J." rather than Evan. On the first weekend in June, 1926, Evan asked Mary, "Yesterday some men in Rushville said they wanted me to run for county sheriff. What do you think?"

"Evan, you are always surprising me. You never talk about political things and always kept your opinions to yourself. And now you are talking about going into politics. Besides when would you have the time to be sheriff?"

"I didn't say yes or no, but lately sales of automobiles have been slow. Most of the business is in repairs and tire sales. I'm not needed for that. I think I can handle doing the sheriff job and sell cars too."

"Well, why did they come to you?"

"They don't think the present sheriff is doing his job and they said I was honest and well-known. They also said I would do a good job."

"Sounds like they were just buttering you up, but whatever you decide I'll support."

"Thanks for the way you have always supported and encouraged me."

Later that week Evan brought home Bill Clark, an influential politician, for supper. It was a complete surprise to Mary and couldn't have occurred at a worse time. She had been busy all day and late that afternoon, when she was preparing the evening meal, she was distracted. Dub had a fight with a neighbor boy. He had a bloody nose and the neighbor boy had a smashed finger. While she cared for the wounded and settled their differences, the roast burned in the oven. She rushed to the kitchen only to find smoke rolling from the oven. It was at that moment that Evan and Bill Clark walked in. "Mary, I brought a friend for supper."

After greeting Mr. Clark, Mary said, "Evan, I need to talk to you for a minute. Mr. Clark, will you excuse us?" In the kitchen she continued, "Evan, I burned the supper. I don't have anything else to put on the table and you've brought a guest home. I am so embarrassed."

"Did you burn up everything?"

"No, just the meat. I think it is edible, but it is black as night on the outside."

"It will be alright, Mary. We'll just say we like our meat well done. Go ahead and put it on the table."

Reluctantly, Mary agreed.

When everyone was seated at the table, Mary expected to hear what Evan had told her in the kitchen. Instead she heard Evan say, "Bill, we have a burnt offering at our house once a week, tonight's the night."

Bill laughed, knowing something unexpected had happened. Mary blushed and explained she had been distracted and allowed the meat to overcook.

"That's alright, Mrs. Furman. I like what E.J. said. In fact, his sense of humor is one reason he would make a good politician."

A month after Evan filed for sheriff, Bill Clark and Sam Johnson went to see him. "E. J., you must get out and greet people. Buy them a cup of coffee or a beer now and then. And putting an announcement in the paper would be a good idea. That's what gets people to vote for you."

Sam added, "You have to sort of butter people up. Get them to like you."

Evan looked across his desk at the two men and said, "Fellows, I have a business to run. I don't have the time to sit around in a restaurant or bar and slap someone on the back. Besides as I see it, people know who I am and my reputation. If they think I would do a good job as sheriff, then they'll vote for me."

"E.J., folks expect politicians to spend time with them and make them feel important. That's what politics is all about. You need to learn to play the game."

"I'll take out an advertisement in the paper, but I'm not going to butter people up or buy them drinks just to get votes. That doesn't seem right to me."

"Suit yourself, but I'm telling you what to do if you want to win this election."

After the election Bill Clark said to Evan, "I'm sorry you didn't win. I thought you would make a great sheriff. Your problem is your principles are too rigid."

"Thanks for your comments Bill. I am not surprised at the outcome. I joke with our kids, "If you can't play a good game, then talk a good game. I must confess I didn't do either in this race. I spent more time on my business and not on what was required to win the race. And honestly, I can't say anything bad about our present sheriff. I think he is a good man."

"E.J., you wouldn't say anything bad about anybody. That's not characteristic of a politician."

"I don't think I'll ever be a politician. But I did enjoy running for sheriff and I met a lot of nice folks."

Announcing

That I have purchased the Fred Anderson garage and wish to invite the public, both old and new customers, to call and get acquainted with the service rendered.

I will continue with a full line of Chevrolet repairs

—Also I will handle BUICK cars and parts and will have some new cars for inspection shortly.

Nicholas Gas and Federal tires will be sold as before.

Furman Garage

E. J. FURMAN, Proprietor
Phone 101

Advertisements courtesy of: Sheridan County Journal Star

CHEVROLET

Its popularity is based on unusual value

The Chevrolet Special Sedan

The introduction of the new Chevrolet Six has established a new standard of value in the low-price field. So evident is its quality, and so attractive is its price, that it is winning a remarkable buying response throughout the country.

In none of the features of the new Chevrolet has there been any compromise with quality. Wherever better materials or improved design could add to the satisfaction and economy of ownership, improvement has been made. See and drive the new Chevrolet Six. It is the Great American Value.

New low prices

Roadster, $475; Sport Roadster with rumble seat, $495; Coach or Standard Five-Window Coupe, $545; Phaeton, $510; Standard Coupe, $535; Sport Coupe, (rumble seat), $575; Standard Sedan, $635; Special Sedan, $650. Prices f. o. b. Flint, Michigan. Special equipment extra.

NEW CHEVROLET SIX

The Great American Value

See your dealer below

Furman Chevrolet, Gordon, Nebr.

Furman Chevrolet, Rushville, Nebr.

ALSO DEALERS IN CHEVROLET SIX-CYLINDER TRUCKS, $355 TO $695, f. o. b. Flint, Michigan

Advertisements courtesy of: Sheridan County Journal Star

CHAPTER 7

Do not pay attention to every word people say

There was a short recession period in the late twenties. Evan was having a difficult time selling any automobiles. He lowered the price as much as possible; still he was not selling anything. In 1928 an ad announced that anyone purchasing a new Chevrolet will be given a spare tire and tube for $1. Finally, he offered to sell if the buyer could only pay half the price of an automobile and would agree to pay the balance within two years.

There were a few people who took advantage of this offer. However, most families believed automobiles were a luxury and if they could not pay cash for one, they would not buy one. Evan's income was reduced, but it did cover all the business expenses and provided a small profit. The family began limiting their spending to just what was needed. The children found the answer to be "no" when they asked for something special. Money was only available for necessities.

Most of the business was in repairs. The ranchers and farmers still needed parts and repairs for their cars and trucks. Evan would make certain the repairs were made, even if the customer could not pay at the time. He had not forgotten the hardships of farming and ranching. He lowered prices where he could, even if it meant no profit.

Calvin Allen, the bookkeeper, said to Evan, "You are extending too much credit to too many people. You're going to be in big trouble."

Evan answered, "These people are good, honest folks. If they say they'll pay, then they will." And they did more often than not; unfortunately it was a dollar or two dollars at a time.

Evan didn't discuss the money problem with Mary. She would ask from time to time if business had improved. Evan's answer was usually, "Today was a little better than yesterday and tomorrow will be better yet."

The short-lived recession ended and people began to have money in their pockets again. Their attitudes changed. They began to want the nicer things in life; to make up for what they had done without. Evan began to sell automobiles again. His offer of 50% down and the balance paid in two years was popular. Evan was reluctant to discontinue the policy.

Automobile sales became the best ever. The family's income exceeded Evan's wildest dreams. Evan's income was averaging over $500 a month. Whatever the children wanted was no longer denied. Mary could again spend money freely.

Jim was in high school and a star on the football team. Early in the fall of his senior year, a man from the University of Nebraska came to watch Jim play. He told Jim that if he was interested in a college education to come to Lincoln and he could attend the University of Nebraska. There would be no tuition charged as long as he played football.

Jim loved football and the idea of playing for another four years thrilled him. He told Evan that night, "A man from the University of Nebraska talked to me today. He said if I played football for them, I could go to school for free."

"So what did you say?"

"I said that would be great. Thank you for the chance to play more football. Just think Dad, I can keep playing football for another four years." The fact that he could get an education at no cost was second to football in Jim's mind. Evan and Mary tried to encourage him to consider the importance of an education. Jim's response was, "Yeah, I know."

Then during the first half of the last game of the season, Jim got hit hard and went down in an awkward position. He got up and finished the half. At half time, he told the coach his leg was hurting, but he thought he could finish the game. The coach told him to drop his pants and they would tape his leg tightly and that would help him. Jim played the entire second half.

The next morning Jim could not put any weight on his right leg; the pain was too great. "Mom, Mom, help me."

Mary went into his bedroom and asked, "What's wrong, Jim?"

"My leg hurts something fierce when I try to stand up."

"How did you hurt your leg?"

"I guess it was yesterday in the football game."

"But you played the whole game. Didn't it hurt during the game?"

"Yes, but only when I ran."

"Did you tell the coach?"

"Yes, but I told him I could still play alright. I didn't want to be taken out of the game."

"Try to move your foot in a circle."

"Wow! That hurts, too. What do you think is wrong with my leg?"

"I don't know, Jim, but you may have broken a bone. We'd better let the doctor look at it. You just lay back down for now. I'm going to get your father."

Mary went back down stairs to the kitchen where Evan was finishing his coffee.

"Evan, I think Jim may have broken a bone last night in that football game. You probably should take him to the doctor."

"Do you really think so?"

"Yes, I do. You go up and see what you think."

Evan went up to Jim's bedroom and after talking with him, agreed with Mary. He helped Jim into some clothes, and then helped him downstairs while being a crutch for his bad leg. "Mary, please call the dealership and tell them I won't be in this morning."

It was painful and a struggle, but Jim made it to the doctor's office, just as he was opening. Evan told the doctor that Jim might have broken his leg in the football game. After examining Jim, the doctor announced, "Yes, Jim's leg is not only broken, the bone is twisted."

"So can you fix it?" Evan asked.

"I can set it and the break will heal but his leg is never going to be the same."

Jim asked, "Can I play football next fall? I plan on playing for the University of Nebraska."

The doctor thought for a minute, searching for the right words.

"Jim, you can go to college next fall, but your leg will not be good enough to play football."

Jim cried out, "This can't be! Please tell me you can fix it."

"I'm sorry, Jim. I'll do the best I can, but I'm afraid your football days are over."

Jim's world came crashing down. "That's not fair. I was going to play for four more years in college!"

Evan said, "Look, son, you can still go to college. I think you should go to the University of Nebraska. Don't worry about the cost; we can work out something to pay for you to go to college."

Jim looked off into space and said, "What good is college if I can't play football? I don't want to go if I can't play. It's not fair. It's not fair."

"Jim, life is not fair. You will not find a promise of a fair or easy life on earth any place, not even in the Bible. As for college, you don't have to decide today. We'll talk about it after your leg heals."

Jim struggled with what he would do after high school. His future had been taken away. He was depressed. His school friends give him varied suggestions and a lot of encouragement.

The newspaper announced "An Old Fiddler's" contest to take place at the Odd Fellow's Hall on January 15, 1929. There would be cash prizes awarded, with first place paying $15.

Roy Davis, who was on the football team with Jim, said, "Jim, let's go see this contest. It ought to be something different."

"You go if you want; I'm not interested."

"Jim, as a friend I'm telling you, I'm sorry you can't play football any more but there are other things in life. You've got to move on." Jim wanted to say, "you are not the one who is losing an opportunity to play football", but he didn't say anything.

Jim slowly began to realize life would go on. It would do no good to wish for what he could not have. As for what to do now, he had no idea. Maybe he would think of something.

The second week of March brought a raging snow storm. The snow had just stopped falling when the County Sheriff called for volunteers to search for a six year old boy who had wandered away from home and was lost. Evan took a pickup truck from his lot and told Jim to join him in searching for the boy. Many men from Gordon joined in the search. After a two day search, no trace of the boy was found. There was nothing more they could do so they stopped searching. Three weeks later when the snow began melting, the boy's body was found two miles from his home.

In summer the talk of the town centered on what was happening in the Black Hills, which was not that far away. This was what was on the mind of John Morse, one of Evan customers, when he came into the garage to have the oil changed on his car. "E.J., have you been reading about some guy carving faces on one of the mountains in the Black Hills?"

"Yes, I read that Congress is giving $250,000 of our tax dollars to chisel out the faces of four Presidents."

"Sounds like you're not in favor of what's going on."

"I don't object to putting Presidents faces on a mountain. That could be a good thing. People might go there just to see it. That could mean more people going through town and more business. I just don't like the government getting involved. When the government gets involved, efficiencies go out the window and politics come in. And I will guarantee you more of our tax dollars will be spent before it is done. Frankly, I would prefer the tax dollars be spent on improving roads."

"I can't disagree with you, E J. How did all this get started?"

"From what I know, Senator Hornbeck and some fellow named Robinson are behind it. Hornbeck got the Senate to approve the money and now President Coolidge is behind it. He wants to have a Democrat and two Republicans as well as Washington on the side of Rushmore."

"Well, that doesn't sound like it will be a political thing."

"Maybe not, John, but I'm guessing the politicians will use this some way to feather their nests."

"Do you really think so?"

"John, the first thought in a politician's mind is, "How do I get re-elected?" That is the difference between a politician and a statesman. A statesman thinks about what is best for the country. Unfortunately, we don't have many statesmen in Congress; we probably never will."

"I heard the Indians are not very happy about it either. Do you think they will cause any trouble?"

"There's nothing they can do except complain about it and no one will pay any attention to what they want. I feel sorry for them. The Black Hills were always special to them."

"Do you think you will go up to see what is going on, E. J.?"

"Probably will someday but I'm not in any hurry. How about you? Are you going to go see it?"

"Yea, I want to go, but I don't know when."

After his leg healed, Jim graduated from Gordon High School. The year was 1928. Right after graduating he went to work for Evan in the parts room at the car dealership. He slowly got over his disappointment and started searching for a different life than what he had thought he would live.

Like his father, he enjoyed dancing and that was still something he could do. But if he was observed closely, his right leg hesitated to certain movements. At a dance one Saturday night, Jim asked one of his schoolteachers for a dance on a dare from Dan Morse, who had played football with him. The teacher's name was Helen Hart. She had just completed her first year of teaching. She loved poetry and often read poems to her English class. Jim was not a poetry lover but he did enjoy hearing Helen read. In her classroom Jim would look at her and think how pretty she was with her auburn hair and dark eyes. Jim had admired Helen and had a crush on her.

Helen accepted his invitation to dance, much to the surprise of both he and Dan. Helen liked to dance and since Jim was no longer a student, she felt there was no problem. He felt awkward at first. Then he felt more relaxed and enjoyed dancing with her. They moved around the dance floor gracefully.

At first the conversation centered on what Jim was going to do now that he had graduated from high school. Since he didn't have any idea what he was going to do he changed the subject to, "What on earth interested you in coming to Nebraska to teach?"

"Money was one reason. The pay is better than I would get in Indiana, where I lived. Nebraska needs teachers, the state even paid for the train ticket out here. As for a second reason, I thought there was some excitement and romanticism in going west."

"Are you sorry you came?"

"Not really, but I do miss some of the things that can be found in the East but not here."

"Like what?"

"Cities and towns are bigger and offer more choices. There are department stores that offer more options in clothing. Actually, there are more options to choose from for most anything."

There was a pause in the conversation so Jim said, "You are a very good dancer."

"Why, thank you, Jim. You are very good yourself." The music stopped.

Jim thanked Helen for dancing with him and said, "Would you dance with me again later?"

"I would be happy to."

Jim walked over to where Dan was standing. "I never thought you would dance with a teacher, Jim. What kind of teacher dances with her students?"

"A very nice teacher and I am not her student any longer. So don't start anything."

Later on Jim asked Helen to dance again and she accepted again. Jim asked if she would be going to any more dances. He told her there was a dance every other Saturday night during the summer. "I suspect that I will since there is not very much to do here, Jim. Do you go to all the dances?"

"I imagine I will. Like you said, there is not a lot to do."

Jim left the dance that night thinking what a wonderful woman Helen was. The thoughts in his mind were, "I would really like to date her, but she is older than me. She could never be interested in me." When Jim learned Helen was going to the Methodist church, he began to attend also. Jim tried to cross paths with Helen every chance he got. Jim and Helen were at every Saturday night dance and spent most of the time dancing together.

Finally Helen said, "Jim, don't you think you would find girls your age more interesting than me?"

Jim knew something would come up about their age difference sometime, but the way Helen asked the question allowed him to express how he felt. "No, I don't. I enjoy being with you much more than girls my age. You are something special."

"Jim, I enjoy being with you. But there is a difference in our ages. I think you should spend some time with younger girls."

"I understand if you don't want to be with me, but I want to be with you."

Helen was at a loss as to what to say. She liked Jim but just never thought of him as a possible suitor. "Jim, I don't know what to say. I am flattered by your feelings, but I feel it would be best for both of us if we spent less time together."

Helen was not at the next Saturday night dance. Jim was facing his second big disappointment in his life, back to back. Evan soon noticed the change in Jim. He still did good work; however, his mind seemed to be on things other than his job.

Since he had taken over managing the parts room, there had been no problems with the mechanics complaining about having the parts when they needed them. Now Evan had overheard one of the mechanics say to Jim, "Hey, this isn't the right gasket. You know that."

Jim answered, "I'm sorry. I'll get you the right one."

Evan walked over to Jim and said, "Something wrong, son? Charlie told me you tried to give him the wrong spark plugs yesterday. Just now I overheard the conversation between you and Sam."

"Yeah, I guess I am kind of messed up. I can't keep my mind on what I am doing."

"After we close up this evening, let's you and I have a talk and you can tell me what's on your mind."

At 5:30 that afternoon, Jim locked the door to the parts room, walked over and sat down at his father's desk. Evan looked at his son and waited for him to speak. There were no customers or any other employees in the show room. Jim took a deep breath and began, "I know this is going to sound silly, but I have a woman on my mind and I can't seem to think about anything else. I try, but nothing seems to work."

"Sounds like you are a love sick puppy, son. Who is the girl?"

"She's not a girl, Dad. It's Helen Hart."

"The school teacher?"

"Yes."

"I'm surprised. How did you ever get involved with her?"

"We got started dancing together and liked being with one another."

"Does she feel the same way?"

"I thought so, but now I don't know. She said I should be with girls my own age. But I do think she likes me."

"Well, there is a big difference in age, Jim. She is older than you are and is probably interested in someone her age."

"I don't know, Dad. One time she said there just weren't many nice single men around here. What do you think of her?"

"From what I have seen and heard, I would say Miss Hart is a fine person. When she said you should be running with girls your age that tells me she is a smart lady as well. Because she is right, you know."

"I just don't see any other girls that I am interested in."

"Well, you have a lot of years ahead of you, and in time you will find someone else to turn your head."

"I keep telling myself that, Dad."

"Just keep on doing it, son. In time it will be better."

The last dance of the summer, both Jim and Helen went. Helen didn't seem to be with anybody, so Jim asked her to dance. "Yes, I would like to, Jim."

"Have you had a good summer, Helen?"

"To tell the truth, I haven't. I must say I have missed spending time with you."

Jim's heart jumped. "I am thrilled to hear you say that. I feel exactly the same way."

"Jim, I don't know if anything serious could develop between us or not, but I am willing to try."

Jim said, "You just made the world seem right again. It will work! I know it will!"

In February of 1930 Jim and Helen Hart were married at Bridgeport, Nebraska. No one knew of the marriage until after it was over. Evan and Mary were the first to be told. Mary said, "Oh, Jim, why didn't you get married in a church here in Gordon?"

"We wanted to surprise everyone and we didn't want people to say anything about Helen being older than me."

Evan said, "You are still going to have that comment to deal with. My advice is to just ignore the issue."

Helen said, "Age difference is not important. It is the two people in the marriage that is important."

"Well said, Helen. Son, I hope you know what a fine woman you have married."

"I do, Dad. I wanted to ask if we could live in the apartment over the garage. It's empty and we could pay some rent money."

"I don't see why not. There's no furniture up there, but I guess you know that."

"Let them have Jim's bed and dresser, Evan, and I have been wanting a new cooking stove, so I'll let them have ours."

"I didn't know we needed a new stove, but OK."

CHAPTER 8

When times are good be happy: but when times are bad, consider; God has made one as well as the other

Evan's second child was Jessie Isabel. She was intelligent and inquisitive. She read a lot and never had to be prompted to do well in school. Most of her school years took place during a period of prosperity, so she lacked for nothing. She had more clothes than most girls her age. She would talk about the latest fashions and what should be worn on special occasions.

Evan would just smile; he wondered what was so important about the clothes a person has. As long as clothes are clean, what else is needed? But Mary understood and would enter into discussions about fashions.

In Gordon High School, Jessie was popular. Since her father had an automobile dealership, she had access to an automobile. This was no small advantage for a high school girl. But it was Jessie's personality that was responsible for her popularity. She dated, but never focused on any one boy.

Early in her senior year, Jessie received a D on an English test. She went home in a huff. Evan asked her what was wrong. "Dad, can you believe Miss. Hart would give me a D on a test?"

"Well, did you deserve a D?

"I did as well as anyone else on the test!"

"I didn't ask what anyone else did. I asked what you did."

"Dad, she is dating my brother!"

"So is she supposed to do something special or make it easy for you?"

"Dad, you don't understand. I want to go to college and low grades will hurt my chances of getting a scholarship or even being admitted."

"I understand you want good grades, Jessie, but you must earn them. I don't think Helen gave you a low grade because she was having a bad day. She gave you the grade she thought your work deserved. Why don't you talk to her tomorrow and ask what you did wrong. All of your grades have been good for the last three years and this D may not be the grade you get for the year."

"I guess you are right. I'll talk to her tomorrow."

"What do you think you would like to do after college, Jessie?"

"Dad, I've been thinking I would like to teach school. That is another reason I want good grades."

"Jessie, teaching sounds like something you would be good at doing. Your low grade on this test just might be a good lesson to remember for when you are a teacher. Where are you thinking about going to college?"

"I talked with my history teacher about colleges and he told me that I could get the education I would need over at the college in Chadron."

"Sounds like you have your mind already made up. Have you thought about what subject you would teach?"

"Not completely. I am thinking about home economics or maybe English. Dad, I know going to college would cost money, but if you could loan me the money to go, I would pay you back after I'm working."

"Jessie, we'll find the money to pay for your college, and don't even think about paying it back. I'd like for all of you kids to go to college. I'm sorry that Jim never went on to college."

The next morning Jessie went early to school to see Helen. "Miss Hart, I want to ask about my test grade."

"I'm glad you want to know about it, Jessie. It wasn't the grade I had hoped to give you, but it was the right grade for your test answers. I think you are capable of better grades. Tell me, how much studying did you do for the test?"

"Not very much; I didn't think I would have to study as much since you are dating my brother. I know now my thinking was wrong."

"Yes, it was. My relationship with your brother will not have any bearing on the grade you receive in my class. I do want you to get the best grade and one you are capable of getting, but you must earn your grades."

"That's kind of what my dad said. I think I have learned something through all this."

Jessie worked even harder her senior year. Foregoing dates and parties, she concentrated on her studies. She graduated in 1929 with outstanding grades. After graduation she applied to Nebraska State Teacher's College in Chadron. She was entering a new phase of life.

Neither Evan nor Mary had graduated from high school. Evan said to Mary, "Our kids are going farther than we did in their education. I am so pleased that Jessie is going to college. Hopefully the other three will go on to college."

Mary said, "Evan, don't try to live the children's lives. I would like to see them go as well but whatever they do, we must support."

"Oh, I will. We are having a good life; I just want them to have a better life than us." Evan's thoughts begin to go back to his teen years and the mistakes he had made. Especially how he had stood up to his father at age 16 and how he thought of himself as so worldly. The thoughts going through his mind were, "The stupid things I did and said back then; I wish I could go back and do things over again. Maybe it's best I can't; I'd probably make the same mistakes all over again or even worse ones."

Evan wondered if he had been successful in raising his children to have a different attitude than the one he had as a young man. He felt Jessie was levelheaded and knew her own strengths and weaknesses. He said to himself, "You just never know if you have been successful or not in raising your children until they are grown, but by then it is too late to correct anything. Now as I look at Jessie, I feel I have been successful, at least where she is concerned."

That fall Evan and Mary drove Jessie to Chadron to enroll in college. As they were returning home, Mary said to Evan, "I think it is wonderful that Jessie is going to college. I wish Jim would have gone, too."

"I feel the same way. You and I never even went to high school and now we have a daughter that not only graduated from high school, she is going to college. Times are changing and education is going to be more important in the future."

Evan's second daughter, Ruth Lucille, was different from Jessie. With only one-year difference in age between the two girls, Jessie influenced Ruth as to what she should wear and what she should do. Ruth's favorite color was blue. She had more blue dresses than any other color. Jessie would tell her, "You can't wear blue every day. You need to buy some other color dresses."

Ruth was somewhat shy and was willing to be a follower rather than a leader. She was also a good student and had a keen mind for bookkeeping and mathematics in general. Whenever Evan would let her, she would go with him to his office. There she would pester the bookkeeper about bookkeeping procedures. Otherwise, Ruth was content to be at home helping Mary with household chores and cooking.

After Ruth graduated from high school in 1930, she decided college was not for her but she wanted to work in an office somewhere. She first approached Evan, "Dad, can I go to work for you? I can keep your books and file papers or anything else you want me to do."

Much to her credit, Ruth never brought up the fact that Dub was working at the garage. Dub was still in school and he did odds and ends around the garage for gas money.

"Ruth, I'm sure you are capable of doing our office work, but I already have someone doing that. I can't just fire them so you can have a job. That would not be right now, would it?"

"No, it wouldn't. But I don't know where to find a place to work."

"Tell you what, Ruth, why don't you go over to the REA office and talk to Mr. Miller. He might be able to use some office help."

"I hadn't thought of that. That's a good idea. I'll go over there tomorrow morning."

Before Ruth went to the REA office, Evan called Ben Miller. "Ben, my daughter is coming to see you this morning about the possibility of working for you. I don't know if you need help or not, but I sure would appreciate it if you would give her some consideration. She will do a good job for you."

"Evan, if she is anything like you, I know she would be a good worker. And as a matter of fact, we will need some help in the Rushville office in a couple of months. Just yesterday I found out our office girl there is pregnant and I'll need to replace her. I'm glad you called me." Ruth went to work for the REA as their office girl in the Rushville office.

Evan told her, "Ruth, you are very fortunate to get this job. Not many high school graduates get offered a job like this one. So do your best and you will keep it."

"I know Dad. I am thrilled to get it. I will do whatever is asked of me."

On graduation day that year, the school dismissed at noon. As the children were going home, a girl crossing the intersection of 5th and Oak Street was hit by a car driven by Paul Turnbull.

A man from the Gordon Journal newspaper, wanting to stir up some controversies, interviewed Evan. "Because of the accident in which the girl was hit, would you say automobile speed in town should be lowered?"

Evan answered, "Most people drive at the speed limit or below in town and the town limit of thirty miles per hour seems reasonable."

"Then you don't think Mr. Turnbull was driving within the speed limit?"

"I have no idea how fast or slow Mr. Turnbull was going when the little girl was hit. I'm very sorry it happened but I have no knowledge of the circumstances. You should be talking with the police, not me."

"Will these kinds of accidents discourage people from buying an automobile?"

"No. Accidents are going to happen. Automobiles do not cause them; people do. If you want to know how to prevent accidents, write about training people how to drive."

The newspaper man was not getting the answers he had hoped for, so he thanked Evan for his time and left.

1930 had begun with some uncertainty in the business world because of the stock market crash a year earlier and some banks beginning to fail. In 1929 stocks were selling for far more than their value. Several investors operated on borrowed money. People began to realize the stocks were not worth what they paid for them, and they tried to sell immediately. Panic developed and stocks quickly became worth next to nothing. Evan told Mary, "I'm glad we don't own any stocks. If we had, we probably would be broke or in worse shape."

Still for the first six months of 1930, Evan was doing well selling cars. He reported selling 33 new cars and 53 used ones in the month of May. Then the bottom dropped out of the retail business as well as all other commerce.

During this time, people had been buying things on credit. The banks did not have enough currency to support the economic situation. People became frighten and tried to withdraw their money from their bank accounts. The banks couldn't cover everyone's withdrawal requests.

The entire United States financial structure collapsed. Businesses went bankrupt in Gordon as well as the rest of the country. As a result, there were several business properties for sale at a very low price in Gordon. The Furman garages did not escape the depressing economy.

People lost jobs and their financial problems mounted. In cities soup kitchens sprang up to provide some food to the desperate. Crime increased due to a lack of available jobs. People looked for anything that might help them forget their troubles, even if was only for a little while. Movies became the answer. In Gordon, people lined up in front of the Pace Theater after an advertisement that read:

Grand Opening for our new sound system
And the picture is, "This is London"
Featuring
Will Rogers.

A sign of the times was the bank robbery at Merriman, Nebraska. Evan had taken a new sedan over to Mr. McLaughlin, the banker in Merriman. He had told Evan he was interested in a new vehicle but wanted to try one out first. While Evan was in the Anchor bank talking to Mr. McLaughlin, three unmasked bandits rushed in the door. They yelled, "This is a hold up don't anyone try to leave!" Everyone held their hands up, including Evan who moved slightly in front of the windows. The town marshal, who happened to be across the street, saw Evan with his hands up. Evan started moving away because the bandits forced everyone into a back room. Then they started emptying the safe. In the meantime the marshal ran into Lessert's Hardware store and grabbed a shotgun off the rack and loaded it and ran back out. As the bandits left the bank, the marshal fired. In the ensuing gun fight, the marshal was hit in the left arm and one bandit lay on the ground seriously wounded. The other two escaped with $7000.

Later, Evan related to Mary what had happened. Mary listened and when Evan finished, she said, "Evan, you could have been shot. I am so glad you were not hurt."

"I don't think those men would have shot anyone. They didn't try to take money from the people in the bank. They just wanted the bank's money."

"People are becoming desperate, don't you think?"

"There are some people that may be as desperate as those fellows but I think those three are just crooks. They would have done this if times were good."

Evan read two months later that Harold Westbrook, alias "White River Whitney" was arrested in the Black Hills and convicted of the bank robbery. He was sentenced to 25 years in prison.

CHAPTER 9

Do not say," Why were the old days better than these,"

In the fall, several of Gordon's business men got together. The conversation centered on what could be done for the town that would encourage people to spend their money. Sam Boyle, who owned the farm implement store, said, "It doesn't matter what we try to do, people don't have any money to spend."

Evan said, "True enough; I don't have any cash either. But you all know people would be buying if they had money. And think about all the business we have done the last few years. I think we owe the town folks something for their past support. Besides, maybe we could give them a day to forget their troubles."

Sam said, "Ok, but what do we do?"

Gilbert Kent, who owned Kent's Cash Grocery store in town, said, "I read the other day about airplanes and how they would be doing all sorts of things in the future. What if we got an airplane to come here for people to see?"

No one was saying anything. Evan had waited to see if anyone else had an idea. No one did. Evan said "That sounds like this airplane idea is something we should look into. Something of the future could give people hope." "You're right E J. I guess we just needed someone to push us."

"Anyone know how we could get in touch with the airplane people?"

Steve Mills, who owned the largest Clothing store in town, spoke up, "My cousin in Omaha wrote to me about an air rodeo that was there in the spring. In talking with some of the pilots, he got to be friends with one of them."

Evan said, "Would you get in touch with your cousin and get a name and address for these folks?"

Steve replied, "Sure. I'll let you all know when I get an answer."

On October 2, 1930, an article appeared in the Gordon Journal that read:

> Air rodeo to take place on Saturday in Jim Barta's alfalfa field south east of the baseball field. There will be no charge, as this is a gift of the Gordon business men. There will be four or more airplanes, including the big tri-motor Ford airplane. Those that are interested in flying can do so at a cost of one cent per pound for their weight.

The first Saturday in October three airplanes landed near Gordon. There was an excited group of people waiting to see them. There was the promised tri-motor Ford, a Curtiss R-6, and a Steirman biplane. The Curtiss R-6 performed loops, rolls, and upside down flying. The audience was enthralled. Rides were offered in the Steirman biplane.

Evan's entire family, including Jessie who had come home for the weekend, were enjoying the day. They were all egging one another to go for a ride in the biplane. Evan and Mary declined, stating they were going to keep their feet on the ground. Jessie and Jim were the only ones wanting to try for a ride. The pilot told Jessie the ride lasted 15 to 20 minutes and he promised no fancy flying. Jessie climbed in and strapped herself down. When she came back she told how you could see for miles and how small people looked. Jim did not get the same promise. When he went up the pilot rolled the plane over shortly after takeoff. Jim was not ready for that and began to get sick. His flight lasted less than 10 minutes. He was glad to get back on the ground.

During the third week of November, 14 inches of snow fell.

This was Ruth's first winter of driving back and forth between Gordon and Rushville. There was one day she could not make it to Rushville. She called her boss to report her unfortunate condition. "Stay where you are; I can't go anyplace either," he told her. She wondered if she should move to Rushville in order to make it to work every day. There had been snow, but the road had always been passable until this time. Then in late December, a snowstorm happened while she was at work. The road to Gordon was closed. No one was going anyplace.

Ruth spent the night sleeping on two chairs in the office when she wasn't answering the telephone calls from customer's wanting to know when their electricity would be back on. Ruth's mind was made up; she must move to Rushville if she was to keep her job. Ruth soon found a widow woman she could room with, so she moved to Rushville during the first break in the winter weather.

One evening in January Evan said to Mary, "In hind sight, I wish I hadn't contributed $50 for that air rodeo. We could use that money now. We are just staying barely in the black at the Gordon garage, and I'm not sure if we will make expenses at Rushville or not. In Hay Springs we're not doing enough business to stay open. I don't know how long we can last if things don't get better soon."

"Evan just be thankful for what we have. Mr. Gordon had to close his jewelry store and now I hear he and his wife may lose their house."

"I heard the same thing. I keep thinking this depression can't last forever. But I don't see any end. I'm wondering what the right thing to do is. There may be financial opportunities now that would pay off in the future. Maybe we should take what cash we have and invest in some of the business properties that are for sale right now. What do you think, Mary?"

"Evan, you know better than I, but spending our reserve cash right now makes me nervous. I think we should hold on to the cash we have. But if you think it wise to buy some building, go ahead. I trust your judgment."

"I understand your feelings, but I think taking a risk now will pay off in the long run. We need to find income from another source or we could go under. The building behind the garage is for sale and if we owned it, we could rent it out for a hardware store or something else."

"Well, if you are wrong, we won't have any money but at least we won't starve. We'll have the food from the garden."

Evan grinned. "Yes the garden is a big help. I remember telling you we didn't need a garden any longer. Was I ever wrong! As for the building I was telling you about, I'm going to make an offer below the asking price. If it is accepted, then I plan to put the title in your name."

"Why on earth would you do that?"

"I've been thinking if something happens to me you need some kind of security. Owning property could give you that."

"Evan, have you been feeling sick?"

"No, but something could happen to me and I just want to make sure you are provided for. Besides, wouldn't you like having some income of your own?"

"I do like that idea."

Evan sold his garage in Hay Springs and closed the dealership. It was with some sadness. Hay Springs had been his first business venture. Out of the 14 years he sold automobiles there, 12 years had been profitable. He thought, "It's not that far from Hay Springs to Rushville, so my customers can drive there for service."

The day of the sale Evan said to Mary, "I'm sorry to leave the Hay Springs garage. I know things change and we must move on with the change, but I feel like I'm leaving a piece of myself there."

"I'm sorry too, Evan. I like Hay Springs; it was our first real house. But like you said, you can't keep losing money. Sometimes a person has to make difficult choices. The garage in Hay Springs will always be special in your memories."

Evan bought the building behind the Gordon garage and was able to lease it to a young doctor who had moved into town. He planned to make it his office.

There were times when Evan had second thoughts about what he had done, especially when their bank account was at zero. Yet they had food to eat and a house to live in. And there was no mortgage to pay. What little cash they had went for utility bills and salaries at the two dealerships. No thought was given to buying anything personal.

One Monday afternoon while Jim and Evan were talking, Dan, the only mechanic left, asked "Do you want me to throw away this split inner tube?"

"Where did it come from?"

"Sam Miller ruined it trying to change a flat tire."

Evan looked at the tube and said, "I'll take care of it." Dan turned and went to pump gas for a customer.

Jim asked, "Why do you want to keep a split tube?"

"I can cut a rubber piece to fit in my shoe. I've got a hole in the sole of my right shoe. I put some cardboard in it but that doesn't keep water out."

"For goodness sakes, why don't you get it resolved?"

"Jim, with Jessie in college, I need every penny to pay for her school. Thank the Lord she got a scholarship, otherwise I don't think she could stay there."

Automobiles were not selling. People did not have money to buy anything, let alone an automobile. Even the service area had very little business. There was one automobile sale that year Evan would always remember. A rancher by the name of Bert Becker needed a small truck in the worst way. He approached Evan one Tuesday morning, "E.J., I've got $250 and I need a pickup. Do you have a used one you could sell me?"

"No, I'm sorry to say I don't have any used pickups. I do have four used sedans and I would sell one to you at a very reasonable price."

"No, I need something I can haul feed and other things. How much for a new one?"

"I've got one for $650. It's a real nice pickup. It has heavy springs and it's even got a heater in it."

"I can't afford that much. Could you sell me something cheaper?"

"I would have to order it from the factory. Let me see what I can do." Evan walked over to his desk and opened a drawer. He pulled out a book that listed both vehicles and parts. After looking at a couple of pages and doing some mathematical calculations in his head, he said, "I'll sell you a plain basic pickup for $510. That's the lowest I can go. You can pay me half now and the balance within two years."

"I don't buy anything unless I pay cash. What would you do if I should die in the next year? No, I guess I'll just wait."

"I hate to see you do that. I will trust you to pay and I don't think you are going to die anytime soon."

"I appreciate your trusting me, but I won't go against my principles." He hesitated, and then said, "I'll make you a counter offer. I'll pay $250 in cash and put up a cow for the other $260."

"I don't take animals on a trade; however, what if you sign a note saying that if you don't pay the $260, then I get the cow. Bert thought about it for a moment, and then said, “Agreed”. They went over to the bank and got a blank mortgage document and filled it out, except rather than listing real estate, there was listed one black cow, four years old.

When Evan got home that night he said to Mary, “I’ve stretched things lately to sell something, but today I accepted a mortgage on a cow in order to sell a pickup.” He chuckled, “But at least I sold something.”

Mary said, “Evan, you are selling more and more on credit. You’re going to wind up with a lot of people owing you money who can’t pay. Then you won’t be able to pay our debts.”

“I know I’m taking a chance on some people, but they are honest, and times are hard. Maybe what I do will help them to get back on their feet.”

Economic conditions did not get better. With no vehicles being sold and people doing their own repairs, there was no cash coming in. Only the few parts that were sold provided any income for the business.

One evening, Evan said to Mary, “This is the first time I have really been worried about money. I have been concerned before, but not worried. It’s a good thing you planted a garden because I don’t have the cash to buy food this month. How long do you think what you have canned will last?”

“We’ve got enough to last through the winter. Then I’ll plant another garden next spring. I only buy flour, sugar, and some coffee once in a while. What really helps us is your brother Leo gave us a half of beef.”

“He has been good to share with us. Did I hear you say you buy coffee only once in a while? How can that be? You make two or three pots of coffee every day.”

“I use the grounds over again. After the morning coffee is gone, I spread the wet grounds out on paper to dry. So the next pot of coffee I make, I reuse the grounds and add just a little new grounds to the old. After the third pot, I use all fresh grounds.”

“I didn’t know we had gotten to that point. I just thought the garden was the reason we weren’t spending much at the store for food.”

“The garden has helped, but with the lack of rain the yield has been less than we usually get.”

"Maybe next year it will be better. I hope we get some good rains by then. It's been so dry. The farmers are in bad shape. Their crops are down to almost nothing. Some of them are quitting and going back east."

"With all the dry conditions, dirt just blows into town every day. I always seem to be sweeping up dirt."

"Mary, I hope you don't think I am complaining about not having any money. I look around and see people a lot worse off than us. We have a roof over our heads and food to eat."

"Evan, when I hear about families without anyplace to live, or standing in line for food, it breaks my heart. I think about those poor families living in cities who don't have a garden to rely on. How do they get enough to eat?"

"I'm not sure they do get enough food. Did you see the article in today's paper about the people in St. Louis almost starving?"

"Yes, I saw it. The Gordon Journal is encouraging people to donate food for people in St. Louis. I think we should give some."

"I feel the same way. I don't have any cash to give but if you have some food you have canned, let's give that. Right now I am thankful we could pay the light bill this month. Fortunately we cleared enough that I could pay everyone's wages this month. We'll just wait and see what happens next month."

"Evan, we are in better shape than most of our neighbors. Why just last week I looked out and saw Mrs. Grimes eying our garden. So I went out to visit with her. She said her garden had not done very well and she didn't know where she was going to get any money to buy food for the winter."

"You mean the widow lady that lives behind us?"

"Yes, I told her to take what she needs from our garden."

"You are a kind woman, Mary. Maybe that's why I married you."

"You don't fool me, Evan. You married me because of my cinnamon rolls."

"Well, that too."

A week later, the Gordon newspaper reported that 50,000 pounds of food stuffs had been collected and was being shipped to relief agencies in St. Louis.

CHAPTER 10

There is a proper time and procedure for every matter

Evan continued going to the garage every day in hopes of selling something. He had in his possession two new automobiles, one used automobile, and three used pickup trucks. He had not ordered anything from the factory for some time. There was no money available.

One was an old Ford pickup that Evan had taken in trade on a new pickup. A rancher had seen it and was interested in buying. Dub was sent out to see if there was any gas in the gas tank.

The gas tank was located in front of the windshield and on top of the engine. Dub stood on the running board and leaned over to look into the tank, but couldn't see anything. He thought he needed some light to see inside the tank, so he lit a match and held it above the mouth of the tank. ***K-BOOM!!*** The fumes ignited and there was an explosion.

Evan and Jim ran outside. There stood Dub with a black ring around one eye and the front of his hair and his eye brows singed. He had the most surprised look on his face. He still held the burned out match in his hand.

Fortunately for him the two ends of the gas tank had blown out rather than the tank blowing up. Jim took one look at Dub and started laughing. Evan had to laugh too. He knew he should say something about the stupid trick Dub had pulled, but he was laughing so hard he could not say anything. Laughs were few and far between, with the economy being so bad.

That evening Evan said to Dub, "You could have gotten yourself killed today. I hope you know that."

"I do now. I just didn't know fumes would come out of the tank and ignite the way it did."

"Fumes are more dangerous than the gas itself. You learned a lesson the hard way. Don't ever have a flame near gas fumes."

"Can the tank be fixed so you can sell the pickup?"

"If new ends can't be welded into the tank, I'll buy a new gas tank. As for selling it, I hope so. We need some cash."

With the business doing poorly, not all expenses were being met on time. They were all covered, just not in a timely manner. Evan decided to sell their house in Gordon and buy a smaller house. "Mary, we can't afford this house and we are in need of cash. If we could sell it, that should provide some financial relief. Could you accept a smaller house someplace?"

"Evan, I will miss this house. But it doesn't matter where we live. Remember, we lived in a soddie when we were first married."

"Well, we won't go to that extreme. I had in mind something like we lived in Hay Springs. Could you accept that?'

"That would be fine. We don't need this big of a house now that Jim and Jessie are not here. Do you think we could sell it? No one has any money."

"There are a few that do and if the price is low enough I believe we could."

After six months and lowering the price twice, the house did sell. Evan found a less costly one in Rushville, so they moved to there. He still owned the Chevrolet garage in Rushville, as well as the one in Gordon. He drove to Gordon every morning hoping something good would happen. Then about noon, he would drive back to the Rushville garage and stay until 6:00.

Business got constantly worse. Evan had to tell Calvin Allen he could no longer pay him. He felt bad about it, but didn't have any choice. It was just he, Jim and Jack Hobson, the mechanic, at the Gordon Garage. At Rushville there was just Dub and one mechanic. The business bank account was depleted and Evan mortgaged the building Mary owned in Gordon. Evan was worried. He had always carried at least $50 in his pocket; now he only had $1. On a Friday morning, Evan called Jim over to his desk, "Jim, I don't know how to tell you this, so I'll just say it. I can't pay you your wages this week."

Jim just looked at his father. "So I'm supposed to work for nothing?"

"Let me finish. I do have enough to pay our two mechanics, but not enough for three salaries. You are family. We can eat at the same table and live under the same roof if we need to, and that might happen. But I can't do that with the two mechanics and their families. Jim, I hope you understand my dilemma."

"I realize the business is in bad shape. I didn't know it was that bad. I'm sorry I spouted off."

"That's alright. It won't make you feel any better but I want you to know, I haven't paid myself for the last three months."

"I didn't know that."

"Well, it is the only thing I could do to hold this minute off." Mary could tell Evan's thoughts and she was concerned about his health. After supper, they sat at the table talking. Finally Mary said, "Evan, why don't you sell one of the garages and concentrate on just one."

"I keep thinking it is going to get better, but it's not. Selling one of the garages sounds like I'm done. I just hate to give up. It makes me feel like I am beat." Evan hesitated, then said, "But maybe you are right. Even if people aren't buying automobiles, maybe we could be profitable if we just focused on one garage. We still sell some parts and a tire once in a while"

"Don't think of it as giving up. You have been successful in what you have done. It's the economic situation; it's not anything you could control."

"Thanks Mary, you always have encouraged me." Evan reached out and squeezed Mary's hand.

Evan notified General Motors that he was going to close the dealership in Gordon if he couldn't find a buyer. General Motors wanted to maintain a presence in Gordon. They contacted the dealer in Denver and suggested he take over the dealership in Gordon.

The Denver dealership was owned by two men, W.H. Brisbane and Frank E. Crane. They had been very successful in Denver and were interested in the possibility of expanding. They drove to Gordon to see Evan and his operation.

"Mr. Furman, we would like to buy your building and the rights to your dealership." Evan thought this was a godsend, yet he wasn't certain that selling the building was a good idea. He would like to keep it because of the income possibilities. He asked, "Would you be willing to just buy the agency and then rent the building from me?"

The two men walked away and began to discuss Evan's proposition. After a few minutes they walked back to Evan.

"We would really like to buy both, but if you are only selling the agency, then we will agree on one condition. That is, if you do sell the building, you sell it to us."

"That's agreeable." Evan continued, "one more condition, will you keep the two employees I have?'

"Yes, they will have a job with us." They shook hands and the Gordon Chevrolet and Buick dealership changed owners in 1931.

Evan now concentrated on trying to make the Rushville garage a profitable business. He was not any more successful in selling any new cars than before. He was able to sell some parts, tires now and then, and gasoline. Dub was helping, but he didn't receive any pay. Evan could not afford to pay anyone.

The income from the garage did cover the building electricity and heating costs; there was very little money to provide for his family. Still he considered himself fortunate when he thought about the farmers and ranchers who were facing mortgage foreclosures. Pessimism was the outlook of most people.

The President, Herbert Hoover, presented his "Reconstruction Finance" plan, which was to aid farmers facing foreclosures. Yet at the same time he said, "Caring for the poor and unemployed was a local and voluntary responsibility." To most people, he seemed to be talking out of both sides of his mouth.

Evan, like everyone else, struggled to understand what was going to happen. He thought, "Thank God for our garden; without it I don't think I could provide food for my family. Yet once again, I paid the light bill."

There was one bright spot in Evan's life. In October, 1931, he became a grandfather. Jim and Helen had a son. They named him James Michael. Evan and Mary were pleased. To Evan it meant his family line would continue.

Jim still worked in the Gordon garage, but under the new owners. His salary was reduced and he was told he would get a small commission on all parts he sold. He and Helen had moved from the apartment above the garage when Evan sold the dealership. They were renting a small two-bedroom house in Gordon. Helen stopped teaching in May. They were struggling to make ends meet with only Jim's income. The house had a small yard with no room for a garden. Without some produce from Mary's garden, they wouldn't have been able to have their own home.

Evan worried and spent more time than the normal working hours, six days a week. There was always a chance that some customer would walk in to buy something. This went on for a year. No matter how many hours a day he was at the garage, it didn't make any difference. The income was minimal.

One night, he began to notice a pain in his chest from time to time, but passed it off as nothing. The next evening after supper, he felt a sharp pain go through his left shoulder and down his arm. He fainted. When he regained consciousness, he was in bed. "Mary, what happened?"

"You have had a heart attack. The doctor said you are to stay in bed and rest."

"I remember sitting in my chair, reading the paper, and then I felt a pain in my shoulder. What happened after that?"

"You passed out and fell out of your chair. I sent Dub for the doctor and he came immediately. Between the two of us we got you in bed. The doctor said you are to do nothing for a month and to take this medicine he left."

"What medicine?"

"One is a hawthorn tincture extract and the other one is Digitalis."

"How long do I have to take them?"

"I don't know. You are to see the doctor in two weeks."

"Mary, I can't lay around for a month. Who's going to handle things at the garage?"

"Dub and Milla, or nobody."

"That isn't going to work. I've got to be there."

"Evan, you are going to stay in bed, even if I have to tie you in it. If you don't take better care of yourself, you could die."

"Oh, alright, I'll take it easy for a while."

"Evan, resign yourself to a longer period than awhile. The doctor said you need to work at something less stressful. I think you should sell the garage."

"Sell the garage! Mary, we have to eat, and Milla and Dub are not even out of school yet. I have to work or we will starve."

"Evan, we'll be alright. Don't think about anything but getting better right now."

After a week Evan was restless. He said to Mary, "I feel as useless as tits on a bull. I've got to do something." Mary would remind him of the doctor's orders. He would chuckle and ask, "Are you my warden?"

Mary would answer, "No, I'm your wife – remember!"

"Not only my wife, but a good looking babe. I think I'll start calling you Babe."

"Evan!"

Evan began to think maybe the business and financial pressure were the reason for his heart problems. Some days later Evan said, "Babe, what if we sold the garage and I went back to raising cattle or farming?"

Mary was a little surprised. She smiled and said, "As long as you don't overwork yourself, it would be fine. We could have a big garden and some chickens. I think we would be just fine."

"Life has some strange twists. I quit farming because I thought I could make more money selling automobiles. And I did. But now I'm talking about going back to farming because I can't make any money selling automobiles. Life is strange. Maybe farming is what I am supposed to do in this life."

Milla, Evan's third daughter, was affected the most by the change in circumstances. She was a junior in high school when they moved to Rushville. Her older brother and sisters lived their high school days during more prosperous times. It was the opposite for Milla. Mary made clothes for her. Her sisters had bought new clothes whenever they wanted. There were no new dresses for Milla.

In the spring of her junior year, Mila was asked to the prom by one of the popular boys in school. That night, she reported her trilling news to Evan and Mary, "Dad, could I have a new dress to wear to the prom?"

"Mila, I would very much like to buy you a new dress, but we simply do not have the money. I'm sorry."

"Well, you found the money to buy Jessie and Ruth a new dress when they went to their prom. It's not fair for you buy dresses for them and not buy me a new dress. The other girls will have new dresses."

"I know it isn't fair, but life is not fair. In fact, life is unfair much of the time. We just have to learn to deal with it. When Jessie and Ruth were in school, our financial condition was better than it is now. It's not that I'm trying to deny you a new dress."

Mary suggested, "Ask your sisters if they have a dress you can wear."

"I'll be the only girl in a borrowed dress."

"Milla, I can assure you the other girls will not have new dresses."

Milla resolved herself to wearing a borrowed dress, even if she thought she would be a misfit.

When Milla got home from the prom, Evan was still up. He asked, "Did you have a good time?"

"Yes, I did. I could have danced some more." She paused. "Dad, you and Mother were right. None of the girls were wearing new dresses."

The following year, when she graduated, Milla wore Jessie's dress to the ceremony. She didn't ask for a new dress. Milla had learned that none of her friends' families had any money to spare. Her brother and sisters had graduation pictures taken, but there was no money for a picture when she graduated. Any thought of going on to college was totally out of the question. Milla had learned to accept what life gave her without complaining.

When he started feeling better, Evan went to the garage every day, even when he knew there would be no sales of parts or anything else. He knew that he would soon have to close the business. The family felt fortunate because they had a roof over their heads and food to eat.

On a hot Wednesday afternoon in July, a stranger stopped his car in front of Evan's garage. He was a government lawyer on his way to the Pine Ridge Indian Reservation to hear complaints about land rights. He walked into the garage looking like he had been mauled by a lion.

Evan asked, "Mister, you look like you need help. What happened to you anyway?"

The man answered, "I'm alright; just scratched up a bit by a dog."

"Did the dog attack you?"

"No. East of here I saw this dog lying down next to the road. I stopped to see if it was alright. When it got up, I could tell it was a fine dog. I thought it must have gotten loose from someone so I decided to put it into my car and take it to town. It bit and scratched me as I put into the back seat."

"Did you find the owner?"

"This is the first place I have stopped. Do you know anyone who is missing a German Shepard type dog?"

"No I don't. Did you say you found this dog?"

The man answered, "Yes, I did. And I had a lot of trouble getting him to settle down,"

"Where is the dog now?"

"He is still in my car, and he acts almost wild. I'll be glad to get him out of my car. I'm afraid he is going to tear it up."

"I'll go out with you and see if I recognize the dog."

When Evan looked in the car he had a hard time stifling a laugh. "Mister, that's not a dog. You got yourself a coyote."

The lawyer's mouth dropped open and he stammered, "Oh my! What should I do now?"

Evan said with a straight face, "Why don't you drive out of town two or three miles, then stop and open the car's back door."

That night he told Mary, "You won't believe what happened today." After he told the story, he said, "That is the best laugh that I've had for a few years."

On March 4, 1933, President Roosevelt spoke on the radio, "Only a foolish optimist can deny the dark realities of the moment." Evan had walked over to the hardware store to listen to the speech on the radio, which had been placed in the center of the sales counter. The volume was turned all the way up. Others were there as well. After the speech, someone said, "A lot of words, but not much on how we can feed our families!"

Evan said, "He is doing what he can. Congress is involved in anything that is done as well as the President. And don't forget, they have only so much money to use; which by the way is our tax dollars. I'm not a Democrat, but I truly think the President is doing what he thinks is best for the country. We just need to help each other and make sure no one goes hungry." Several heads nodded in agreement.

In a subtle way Evan began inquiring all over the county about the possibility of selling the Rushville dealership. A year later, one of the people he talked with was Emery Ogden, who owned a garage in Batesland. Emery told him that Arthur Richards, who lived near Martin, South Dakota, had approached him about buying his garage. "I told him I wasn't interested. I wanted to continue repairing automobiles."

Evan thought for a minute, and then said, "Did you ever think about selling them as well as repairing them?"

"Sure, but my building is not big enough for show room and doing repair work. Besides nobody is buying right now."

"What if I sold you my garage in Rushville? It's big enough to sell and repair automobiles."

"Why do you want to sell your garage?"

"I had a heart attack and the doctor said I should do something different. So I was thinking about raising cattle. Now if Mr. Richards owns land, and he trades you land for your garage, then I'll trade you my garage for the land."

"Sounds like something I might be interested in, E.J. Tell you what, I'll talk to Mr. Richards and see what he owns and if he would be interested in such an arrangement."

A week later Emery walked into the Rushville garage. Dub was sitting behind the counter. "Is E.J. Furman here?"

"Not right now, but he should come in before long. He usually is here between 10 and noon. His health has not been very good so he doesn't spend much time here. Is there anything I can do for you, mister?"

"No, thanks. I want to talk to him about some business. When he comes in, tell him Emery Ogden wants to see him. I'll be over at the cafe drinking coffee."

When Evan came in, Dub told him about Emery. Evan walked across the street to the cafe and joined Emery. He said, "Arthur Richards owns a section and a half east of Martin, South Dakota.

I told him your suggestion. He thought it was a good idea. He is agreeable to a three-way deal. If a section and a half would satisfy you, we can all three make a deal."

A deal was worked out in the summer of 1933. None of the three parties had any cash, so just real estate changed hands. Evan did take a new sedan and was able to sell two other automobiles to the Gordon dealers.

There was now no reason for Evan and his family to stay in Rushville after the three-way sales transaction. The section and a half of land he acquired when the garage in Rushville was sold had a house and barn as well as a few other out buildings. They put their house in Rushville up for sale. Evan did not receive as much cash for the Rushville house as he had hoped for but he felt the price was fair.

After graduation Milla went to work as a waitress in a cafe in Rushville. She continued to live with Evan and Mary until they moved. She paid them what little she could. When they moved, she stayed in Rushville and moved in with Ruth.

CHAPTER 11

Words from a wise man's mouth are gracious

Evan, Mary and Dub moved to their new property five miles east of Martin, South Dakota. Evan went back to raising cattle and farming. The house was in a valley close to the road going into town. There was a big garden between the road and the house. The house had three bedrooms, living room, and a nice size kitchen. The best part as far as Evan was concerned was the enclosed porch that was across the entire front of the house.

There was a creek behind the barn that turned south at the end of a pasture. Trees lined both sides of the creek, which provided natural protection for the cattle in the winter. The property consisted of one and a half sections of land. Indians owned most of the surrounding land. Evan was in hopes he could lease some of the Indian owned land.

All of Evan's available relatives helped in the move. After the last chair was put into place, his brother Leo asked, "What are you going to do about animals and equipment?"

"I am going to see if I can borrow some money. When the house in Rushville sells I can repay the loan. If I can't borrow, then I'm very limited in doing anything. Right now I am just thankful we have a roof over our heads."

"Evan, let me help. I owe you for you helping me when I needed it. I'll sell you 20 cows and loan you a bull. You can pay me when you have the money. Also, I can loan you a couple of horses and I know we have a hay rake and a few other things we are not using."

"Thank you, Leo, that is very kind of you; I'll take you up on your offer. That will be a start."

"Listen, Evan, you have done much more for me. You have looked out for me ever since I was a baby. I don't think I'll ever know what all you have done for me."

"I haven't done much and what I did do was because mother told me to look after you."

"Ok, but you are going to need more than the help I provide. Maybe you can buy some equipment at one of the auction sales. There seems to be one every week, with so many folks quitting farming and cattle raising."

"I plan to go to an implement sale down at Merriman this Saturday. I would like to find a tractor, but it would have to be cheap. Then maybe I can buy some heifers at the next livestock sale"

"Not too many tractors in the sales I've been to, but maybe you can find one. I'll find someone to truck the cattle over to you. It may take a week."

"Leo, it has been awhile since I made my living from the land. Have I done the right thing or am I headed for a fall?"

"No one knows what the future holds, but you'll make it. The Furmans always have."

Before a month ended, there were some cattle, hogs, and chickens on the place. Evan and Dub had arranged things more to their liking and repaired the fences in a few spots. When Evan went into the house at the end of the day, Mary would fuss over him. She warned him about overdoing things.

"Mary, I'm fine. The sunshine and fresh air do marvels for me."

They still did not have a tractor. This bothered Evan; he had found one but the price was more than he could afford. He was trying hard to be patient. He also wanted to build a better barn when money became available. He told Dub, "I get frustrated because I don't have the cash to buy what we need. But we have made good progress in just a month. Let's hope it will continue." Not all was good. There had been strong winds in 1933 and because of the drought conditions soil had blown away. Then on November 11th a series of dust storms began which would last through the winter and into the next spring. One storm lasted for two days and topsoil blew all the way to Chicago.

The first Christmas in their new home was 1933. Evan and Mary wanted all the family to come for Christmas dinner. The girls were grateful for the chance to visit with everyone; and for the meal, since none of them could afford to buy anything special for a Christmas meal.

Ruth brought her fiancé, Roy Andrews, to the dinner. It was the first meeting for the family. Roy started a conversation with Evan about politics. "Mr. Furman did you know that the Nebraska legislature passed a bill establishing only one house rather than two houses?"

"Yes, I heard about it. It's not something new. Back in 1919, when I almost went to a constitutional convention, it was discussed and came close to passing. People have tried a couple of times since then."

"Why didn't it pass back then?"

"Politics; there was a tie vote at the convention and the convention president broke the tie by voting no. The legislators in office at that time were afraid they would lose their positions so they put pressure on the president to vote no."

"Well, do you think it is a good thing to have only one house in the legislature?"

"It should save money and should take away the hassling between the two house conference committees on differences in bills that passed."

"The way you are talking, I can't tell if you are a Democrat or a Republican."

"Roy, you shouldn't ask folks what their politics are, but I'll tell you a story. A few years ago Mary and I were driving to Chadron when we got stuck in a big mud hole. I couldn't get out. A man came along with a team of horses and offered to pull us out of the mud. I gladly accepted his offer. Then just before he hitched the horses to the front of the automobile, he asked me if I was a Democrat or a Republican. I told him I was a Republican. He never said a word. He just left us stuck and went on his way. A second man came along on a tractor and offered to help but before he hooked a chain to the automobile, he asked the same question. I gave the same answer; and he drove on. When the third fellow came by, I said we were Democrats. He pulled us out of the mud and we started visiting. Well, it was a hot day and the man suggested that one of the watermelons in the patch on the other side of the fence would taste good. I agreed and crossed over the fence. I took out my knife and bent down to cut the stem off a nice looking melon. Before I did, I thought to myself, "I have only been a Democrat 15 minutes and I'm stealing already."

Roy, who was a democrat, didn't like the story but said nothing. He just turned and walked away. He never discussed politics with Evan again.

Jim and Helen were the last to leave. Jim wanted to talk to Evan. "Dad, I don't know what we're going to do. I lost my job and I can't find any work. I have asked every place I can think of. I can't buy Helen and Mike anything for Christmas. I don't have any money. Helen talked to the school principal about teaching but they won't hire her because she is married and has a son. Do you know anyplace I could work?"

"No, I don't; wish I knew of something. You could throw in with us. We won't get rich, but we won't starve either."

"Thanks for the offer, but we both know two families under the same roof is not a good idea."

"Look Jim, we have a lot of land. We could build you another home. You don't have to live in the same house with us."

Jim looked at Helen, "What do you think?"

"Jim, I don't think we have much choice. You know we don't have any money to pay the rent for next month."

"If Ma doesn't mind, we'll try it."

"She'll think it is great, especially with little Mike being here."

As soon as the ground thawed, Jim and Dub started digging a basement not very far from Evan and Mary's house. The plan was to put a roof over the basement and divide it up into three rooms. This was the least costly way to build a house. Jim and his family moved in with Evan and Mary. There were good relations between the two families, but very little privacy. The three men spent most of each day building a basement house for Jim and Helen.

Milla was living the life of a single girl. She continued to work in the Rushville cafe. One of her regular customers at the cafe was a young man named Larry DeWitt. He was fortunate enough to have work so, he had some money. It was not uncommon for him to have a different girl for his dining partner when he came to the cafe on Saturday nights. Three months later he would always eat alone. Milla thought, "Well, he must have run out of women." Then Larry asked Milla for a date. She told him no, she wouldn't even consider it.

Larry kept asking, "Milla, I'm not a bad guy. Why won't you go to a movie with me?"

"I don't think you know what you want in life. Look at all the different girls you have dated."

"So I've dated a lot of girls; does that make me a monster?"

"Larry, I'm just not interested in you. So forget it."

This became a challenge for Larry. He kept asking Milla for a date. Finally, Milla decided that if she went out with him once he would leave her alone, so she agreed. They went to a movie and Milla confessed to herself that she did have a good time and didn't have to pay to see a picture show.

Two weeks later Larry asked her again for date. Milla hesitated, and then said OK. A third time became a fourth time and it wasn't long until they were constant companions. Larry decided Milla was the right woman for him. He asked her to marry him. Milla looked at him when he presented her with a ring. "Who else has had this ring on?"

Larry was surprised at her question. "What are you talking about? You just can't forget about the other girls I dated, can you?"

"No, I can't. How could I be sure that you would be satisfied with just me or if you would continue going after other women after we married?"

"You are the only woman I want to spend the rest of my life with, and you need to believe that."

"I don't know. I won't say yes and I won't say no right now. I'll give you an answer this weekend." Milla wanted to talk to her Dad. He was good at judging people and he had always given her good advice. However, in order to talk to him she would have to go to Martin, South Dakota.

Milla borrowed Larry's car and drove to her parents' place. Evan and Mary were surprised by her visit, but glad to see her. After telling them all the news of the happenings in Rushville, Milla continued, "Dad, Larry DeWitt asked me to marry him."

"Well, are you going to?"

"I don't know, Dad. What kind of a person is he?"

"As far as I know he is a good, honest person. He has a reputation of keeping his word. And I don't think he is lazy. He has always had a job to my knowledge."

"So do you think I should marry him?"

"Milla, that is for you to answer, not me. Do you love him?"

"Yes and no. I do enjoy his company, but I keep thinking about all the other girls he has dated."

"Milla, don't let that be the deciding factor. Think of it this way, out of all the girls in Rushville, he has chosen you to be the one he wants to spend the rest of his life with. You are the important one to him."

"I never thought of it that way. It does seem different when I think of Larry like that. Thanks, Dad. Maybe he is the right one to marry."

"Well, whether you marry Larry or someone else, I do have a request."

"What's that, Dad?"

"Mary and I never got to see Jim or Ruth get married. We would like to be present at your wedding whenever it is."

"Dad, I promise, you and Mom will be there."

Before the summer was over, Jim, Helen and Mike moved into the basement house. Jim and Helen were very grateful for Evan and Mary taking them in, but Jim couldn't help but hope for a place of their own.

One year later, Jim learned of a half section of land with a house that the bank wanted someone to take over. The bank already had more parcels of land they had foreclosed on than they knew what to do with. No one had the money to buy land. The banker told Jim, if he would take over the place he would only have to pay the interest for the first two years.

Jim was excited. He told Helen, "This is our chance. We may never get an opportunity like this again."

"But Jim, your Dad and Mother have helped us and given us a place to live. We can't just walk out now."

"I know and I appreciate all they have done, still I don't think they would hold us back. What if I talk to Dad about it?"

"You talk with him. If he thinks we should do it, then what can I say."

That evening, Jim walked over to the main house and found his Dad setting on the porch. "Dad, I need to talk to you about an opportunity."

"Sit down and tell me what's on your mind."

"Helen and I are indebted to you and Ma for taking us in and giving us a place to live. I don't know what we would have done if you hadn't helped."

"Jim, families help one another when the need is there. You may need to help us some day. But I don't think saying thank you is what is on your mind."

"No, it isn't. It's about the possibility of owning our own place."

"I hope you can find a place to call your own. It will happen someday."

"That someday might be now. We have a chance to own a half section down on the state line."

"Where are you going to get the money?"

"That's the good part. The bank seems to be holding more land titles than they know what to do with. When I was in the bank yesterday, Mr. Green asked if I would be interested in a proposition. He told me about the section of land with a house on it that the bank needed to sell or get someone to take over. He said if we agreed to pay just the interest on the loan twice a year for the first two years, we could move in. Then after the two years we would have to pay both principle and interest."

"Jim, it does sound like an opportunity, but where are you going to get cows and equipment? I'm not in any position to help you."

"I know and I'm not asking for you to stake us. I'm only asking how you would feel about Helen and me moving out after you provided us with a house and food."

"I think your moving to a place of your own is fine. Ma and I would not hold you back. I just don't know if you can get a place going with conditions being the way they are."

"Dad, I know it will be a struggle, but a chance like this does not come along every day and I want to take advantage of it."

"If that is the way you feel, then try it. I can share equipment with you for a while but that's about all the help I can offer."

"Thanks Dad, I told Helen you would be supportive."

Jim and Helen moved onto the half section of land. The house was livable but in need of repairs. The only livestock they had were three heifers Jim had gained from helping his father, one sow they were given, and a dozen chickens. Jim asked Leo if he would sell some cows or heifers and wait for a while to get the payment. Leo was glad to help.

The first year went well enough. There was a good wheat crop and 15 calves were born. Jim was excited and full of energy; Helen did not feel the same. Still, she adjusted and encouraged Jim. Before 1934 ended, she was pregnant. The winter was cold and provided more than normal snow. They felt renewed when spring arrived; however, the spring rains didn't arrive. Without the rains, dirt began to blow. The land had been over farmed and over grazed for the last five years. There was not enough vegetation to hold the ground in place. From time to time dust storms would occur and sometimes last all day. The air would be so full of dust that visibility would be no more than ten feet.

Such a day was March 13, 1935. The day started out hot. At 5 p.m. it had cooled down to 86 degrees. Just before 8 p.m., the dust storm started. The wind was fierce. Dust particles filled the air. The nighttime stars could not be seen. It was an eerie darkness. People stuffed rags, towels, even blankets in every crack and hole in the outside walls of their homes. Still the dust seeped inside; it came down chimneys and around doors and windows. If someone opened a door, the dirt would pile up before the door was closed.

As if Mother Nature felt compassion, the temperature started falling. By midnight it was 30 degrees and snowflakes began to replace the flying dust. The next morning the temperature was 18 degrees. But the blessing was that there was four inches of snow on the ground covering the dirt. The unseasonable heat wave was broken. The bad side was the clean-up process that was required to make the house livable again.

The relief was only temporary. Dust storms returned in May and June. Several times the sun was completely blotted out by blowing dust. One of the worst dust storms in history occurred on April 14, 1935. The day would be remembered as 'Black Sunday'.

After such a storm, Helen would sweep and scoop dirt out of

the house. It would blow in through cracks and even the keyhole in the door. Everything in the kitchen had to be washed. Curtains, blankets, and clothes also had to be washed. Mary was doing the same at their house. The problems caused by the dust storms were worse than any caused by blizzards in the winter.

Evan would contact Jim and his sisters after these storms to find out how they survived. After a May storm, when Evan drove to Jim's place, he could see Jim was discouraged. In an effort to cheer him up, Evan said, "We have one God-send, Jim. The Federal Government is going to buy cattle for $18 a head. That's more than we could get at the auction."

"Why are they going to do that?"

"Well, as I understand, they are trying to help us because they know we can't afford to feed cattle and they don't want all of us to go bankrupt. The animals they buy will be put into a relief program and distributed to families in need."

"That sounds good for you, but I don't have enough steers to sell so how's it going to help me?"

"Jim, whatever cattle you can sell, I'll include with my steers and you will receive the money for them."

"Guess I can do that. I will have two maybe three this fall. That will provide more cash than I've seen in a while."

Furman place located east of Martin, S.D.

CHAPTER 12

No man has power over the wind to contain it

The struggles through the depression and the harsh weather continued for the Furman family. Their situation was no different than anyone else. Evan's children were accepting whatever life gave them. Each day brought something different to each of Evan's offspring.

Jessie had done well in college and graduated with honors in 1935. She was hired to teach Home Economics in Torrington, Wyoming, when school started in the fall. Evan was proud of her. He said, "Mary, isn't it great that we have a daughter graduating from college! I knew she was capable and now she knows it too. Believe me, she will be a good teacher."

While she was in college, she met a young man named Gerald Chambers. They became very friendly. Jessie thought his name was a bit formal, so she started calling him "Chick". This nickname would stick with him for the rest of his life. Later in 1939 they would be married.

Jim was about to experience being a father again. One hot day in mid July, he and a neighbor, Bob Baker, were rebuilding a fence that divided their properties. They were short a fencepost. Jim said, "I have two or three posts behind the shed by our house. Since you have your truck here, would you mind driving to our house and getting a post?"

"Sure, it won't take more than 10 minutes for me to go and come back."

"I'll staple the wire we've strung to the posts we've set while you are gone." As the neighbor drove past their house, Helen, very pregnant, came out somewhat bent over. She waved and said, "Am I glad to see someone. I didn't know what I was going to do. I need to get into town. The baby is coming." Just then she winced in pain.

"I'll go after Jim."

"I don't think there is time. You had better get me to the hospital first."

"Alright, get in." Bob flew down the road with the dust rising behind his pickup.

They never made it into town. Helen's labor pains were happening faster and closer together. When Helen screamed in pain, Bob stopped at the first house they passed. An Indian, who was well respected, owned the house and his wife was a midwife. After they got Helen inside, Bob went back after Jim.

Jim wondered why Bob had been gone so long. Then he saw him coming across the pasture faster than he should be going. "What's happened?" Jim yelled as he ran up to Bob's pickup.

"I started to take your wife to the hospital, but we never made it to town. I stopped at Big Jake's place. Her baby is about to be born! Bob was as excited as if his wife was having the baby. He repeated, "Your wife is having a baby right now! Come on, I'll take you there."

Jim got in the truck. "Thank goodness Mike is at Dad's. I guess Ma knew what was going to happen when they came over to get him two days ago. How's Helen?"

"I can't say. She was yelling from time to time. I could tell she was really hurting. I left to get you as soon as we got her into the house." The two men went faster than was safe across the prairie to the road and then on to Big Jake's house with the dust rolling up behind the pickup. As Jim ran in the house he heard a baby cry.

A red headed boy was born just before Jim got there. Evan would always say the reason the boy's hair was red was because he was born in an Indian's house. Helen was tired but well. Jim kissed her while he held his new son. "You just rest now and when you feel like it, I'll take you home."

Helen closed her eyes and mumbled, "OK". She was soon asleep. Jim took his new son out to show Bob and asked if he would take him back to his place to get his truck.

Bob answered, "Sure. Do you want to take that fine-looking boy?"

"Heavens no, I just brought him out to show you. I'll take him back in and thank Jack's wife for her help. Give me a couple more minutes then I'll be ready."

That evening they returned home. Jim did his best to cook something to eat. After their meal of eggs and coffee, he washed and put away the dishes. Helen and the baby were asleep. Jim walked outside and looked at the sky. It was clear.

He said to the sky, “Lord, I sure could use your help. I’ve got a bigger family to provide for. We need rain or there won’t be a wheat crop to harvest or any hay for the winter. It is so hot and dry. Guess I should be thankful the well hasn’t gone dry. At least there is water for us and the livestock.” He looked around and thought, “Yeah, and while I’m being thankful, I must not forget to be thankful for Mom and Dad sharing their garden produce.”

The next morning, Jim and Helen discussed what the baby’s name should be. Helen wanted the name, Charles Patrick. Jim wasn’t so sure, but he didn’t have any other suggestion. Later that day, Evan and Mary walked in. They brought Mike back home and they wanted to see their second grandson. Evan asked, “What’s his name?”

Jim answered, “Helen wants to call him Charles Patrick.”

Mary said, “The way you said that it doesn’t sound like you’re so hot on the name.”

“Oh, it’s OK I guess. I can’t think of anything better.”

Helen looked at Jim, “I didn’t realize how you felt, Jim. I thought you liked that name. It doesn’t have to be Charles Patrick.”

Mary said, “Have you thought about naming him after one of his grandfathers?”

“That’s a good idea, Mom. Helen, why don’t we name him after both his grandfathers?”

“I like that thought, Jim. His name will be William after my father and Evan after your father.”

Evan didn’t say anything during the discussion and he wouldn’t now. But it was obvious from the look on his face that he was pleased to have a grandson named after him.

Mike looked at the new baby and asked, “Did you get him out of the Montgomery Catalog?” He blushed when everyone started laughing. Mike looked at his Dad and then at his Grandpa, Evan. He was searching for an answer. Evan sat down and put Mike on his knee. Then he said, “The best explanation I can give you is, your Dad planted a seed under your Mother's heart and the baby grew from that seed." That seemed to satisfy Mike.

Jim said," Thanks Dad, I didn't know how to answer Mike."

On the way home, Evan said to Mary, "Babe, I never thought I would have someone named after me. Sure sounds good and makes me feel good. Kind of like after I'm dead, my name will still be spoken and I won't be forgotten." Evan and William Evan would always share a special connection.

There was only one rain from the time William Evan was born until October the first. The result was there was not enough of a wheat crop to harvest and very little hay for the winter. Jim and Helen's garden dried up. There was nothing they could can or save for the winter. His father and mother's garden prospered because they could water it from their well, which was the best well in the area. Evan would come by from time to time and bring fresh vegetables. The moisture did finally come, but in the form of snow. It was a winter of above average snowfall.

At Christmas that year, Mille announce that she and Larry Dewitt were going to get married.

"When Milla?" Evan asked.

"We would like to this weekend if you would allow us to do it in your living room."

"Thank you for remembering my request."

Mary said, "Of course you can if you don't mind being married in a house that might not be clean."

"Mother, I have never seen your house when it was not clean. It will be fine. We don't plan on inviting people so don't think about doing anything special."

Three days later, Milla and Larry drove over to Martin. They stopped in town and got the Methodist preacher, then went on to Evan and Mary's house. Evan, Mary, Jim, Helen, and their two boys were waiting for them. Evan said, "Babe we're finally going to see one of our children get married. That makes this day special."

After they said their vows and received their congratulations, Mary announced, "Dinner is ready." It was a joyous meal even though it was sparse. While they were eating, the snow began to fall. Larry said, "Milla, I know you would like to stay and visit, but we had better go while we can. I don't know how bad the roads might get."

Evan said, "You are welcome to stay here if it starts to get bad."

"I know Dad, but Larry is right. We had better go or we could get caught here or some place in open country. You know sometimes it takes days to get the roads back open after a snow storm and we both have to be at work Monday."

As they said their goodbyes and started to leave, Mary said, "Just a minute you two. Take some of this leftover dinner with you." They drove away with the snow beginning to cover the ground. They dropped the preacher at his house and gave him $2 for performing the marriage ceremony.

The snow continued to fall, yet there was no trouble until they were just west of Gordon. The snowfall became heaver and the wind speed increased. The snow seemed to be going horizontal rather than vertical. The visibility was horrible; you could only see three feet in front of the car. Larry had driven this road many times and had a sense for where the road actually went.

"Larry, do you think we will make it to Rushville?"

"Sure we will." In his mind he was not so sure. He had slowed the car another 5 miles per hour. With the visibility so bad, going any faster would be dangerous. Yet he knew if he stopped they would be trapped so he kept the car moving. They had not seen another automobile for over an hour.

Milla slid closer to him and put her arm around him. "I do trust you. Still I have got to say, I hope you are right. I don't want to spend our wedding night in somebody's house that I don't know; or worse, in this car."

It seemed like an eternity to both of them before they saw lights of Rushville. Their spirits were raised. Larry squeezed Milla's hand. "We're going to make it." 20 minutes later Larry stopped the car in front of the house where he had been living. They both ran into the house closing the door behind them and sinking to the floor. Milla silently said, "Thank you Lord."

After Milla and Larry left, Evan said to Mary, "Babe, our children are leaving us and starting homes and families of their own. We must be getting older. Funny, I don't feel like I'm an old man and a grandpa."

"Well, you're not old yet; at least you weren't last night when we were in bed."

"Well I'm not dead yet."

The economy did not improve and the rains still did not fall. Evan and Mary managed to maintain what they had. Dub lived with them and worked with Evan. Jim and Helen seemed to be struggling more than the girls. Jessie was teaching and had an income. Ruth was married and had the security of a weekly paycheck. Milla and Larry seemed to be alright even though Milla lost her job as a waitress. Larry had a paying job and had become a volunteer fireman.

In January 1936 Evan's father died. Larry DeWitt drove over to tell Evan the news. When Evan heard the news, he was determined to make the trip to Rushville where his father had lived. He said to Mary, "We have got to go to the funeral. I'll follow Larry back to Rushville."

"Evan, the weather looks threatening and there is more than 6 inches of snow on the ground. You could get caught in a storm."

"I know but I want to show respect for my father. We didn't always agree on things, still I always respected him. He taught me what was important in life. I need to say good-bye to him."

"If you are that determined to go, then I am going with you."

"I knew you would go and I appreciate your willingness to go. I'll gas up the car and put some water in a jug for the trip. Maybe I had better put a shovel in the car, just in case. Let's leave in half an hour, if Larry is agreeable."

"That's fine with me. The roads were OK coming over but who knows what they will be like an hour from now. If anything goes wrong we can help one another."

"Can you be ready, Babe?"

"I'll be ready and I'll bring some blankets."

They made the trip under cloudy skies and blowing snow. Evan stopped in Martin to telephone that they were on the way. When Evan returned to the car he said, "They are going to wait until we get there for the funeral service."

After the funeral, the family gathered at the stone house on the

Furman ranch. There was a lot of reminiscing of days gone by. Some of the conversation was about how everyone was struggling through the depression and dust storms. Evan went outside to smoke and Leo went with him. Leo said to Evan, "Sometime this summer, I'll swap bulls with you."

"You don't need to do that; just come and get the one you loaned me. He is yours. I do thank you for the loan. He was a big help in getting us started in building a herd."

Leo continued, "He is a young bull that I hadn't used yet. I'm glad you could use him. But now our present bull has been with our cows for five years and we need to bring in another. So let's swap. We both will have new blood introduced into our herds. Just how is your herd doing?"

"I don't think it could be called a herd yet, but we are up to 50 cows and last fall we sent 40 calves to market. This year we hoped to send 45 calves and add at least four or five heifers to the herd."

"How is Jim doing on his place?"

"He's struggling. There is no natural shelter for his cows and the soil is too sandy to raise much of anything. We give him what help we can."

"I hope he makes it. Let me know if I can do anything."

Evan and Mary were not doing great financially, but they were doing better than many others. Besides selling calves once a year, they sold a wheat crop. They also started raising turkeys, which sold well at Thanksgiving and Christmas times. Chickens contributed to their income, as well as providing eggs to sell or trade. Plus the chickens contributed to their own food supply. Mary's garden provided plenty of vegetables and she canned enough to last through the winter, so food was not a problem for them.

Evan wanted to increase their ownership of land but without any cash, it was out of the question. He wanted more land so he could plant wheat or oats and still increase the number of breed cows. Without access to more land this would be impossible.

Even if there had been money, it was unlikely that any land could have been purchased, since Indians owned the surrounding land. The Indians were wards of the U. S. Government, which meant the Government would be involved in any land transactions.

Evan said to Mary, "We can't buy more land so maybe we could lease some."

"Good luck on doing that."

He learned the names of two people who owned adjoining land, both were Indians. Evan hoped he might lease their land. When spring weather allowed travel, he began his search for the Indian landowners. Indians had a habit of moving around during the summer, but normally stayed in a house during the winter. Before he started though, he needed someone to go with him.

Mary suggested, "Why don't take Mike with you. He probably would like driving around." Evan went over to Jim's place and asked if Mike could accompany him. Jim said yes and Mike was thrilled at the thought of riding around the countryside with his Grandpa.

Evan found both land owners without much trouble. He found the first owner at the place he had been directed to. The first owner was Mary Whitebelly, an older widow who still lived by herself. After Evan explained the reason for his visit, she asked, "Did you sell automobiles and trucks in Nebraska?"

"Why yes I did, but I am not doing that anymore."

"I have heard of you. You sold a truck to my brother when he did not have all the money to pay for it. You trusted him."

"What was your brother's name?"

"Hank Lonetree. He said you were a good man."

"I do remember him and he paid me every cent he owed for the truck."

Mary then asked, "How much will you pay me to lease my land?"

"I don't have much money. I will try to pay you $100 every year."

"That is not very much."

"No it's not, but I can't pay more. How much are you getting now for the Land?"

"Nothing."

"So isn't $100 better than nothing?"

Mary looked at Evan then said, "I will lease the land to you. Will you draw up the paper?"

"Yes, I'll write out an agreement and sign it. I'll get someone to witness it so it is legal and bring it back."

"My brother said you were an honest man so I will trust you. Just sign a paper now. You don't need to come back."

Evan wrote out that he would pay $100 dollars a year to Mary Whitebelly for the use of one half section of land that had a common boundary with his property. The common boundary was his north property line and Mary's south property line. It was not really a legal document but Mary was satisfied, and Evan thought it would be sufficient.

He moved on to find the next owner who took longer to locate. When he discussed the reason for the visit, he received a cold reception and was turned down. As Evan returned home, he said to Mike, "It is just as well that I only got one lease signed. I'm not sure there would have been enough money for another lease. But I do have enough money for us to stop and wet our whistle. Would you like to do that?"

"I'm kind of thirsty, Grandpa. Could I have a Coke?"

"Sure."

Evan stopped at the M & M bar. He and Mike sat at a table with two other men that Evan knew. Evan ordered a beer for himself and a coke for Mike. Mike sat quietly in his chair, eyeing Evan's beer. Evan stopped talking to the men when he noticed Mike looking at his beer. He said, "Mike, do you want a drink?"

Mike answered, "It looks good. Yes, I would like to taste it." One sip was enough; Mike didn't want anymore.

When they got to Evan's house, Mike informed Mary, "I didn't like that drink that Grandpa gave me."

Mary looked at Evan, "What did you give the boy?"

"I just let him taste my beer."

"I can't believe you. Mike is only six years old. Are you planning on introducing all your grandchildren to beer?"

"Now, Babe, don't get upset. It didn't hurt him. But I won't do it anymore if you are going to get upset."

The year brought more rain than they had seen over the last two years. Still there was still a shortage of rainfall. The little stream behind the barn, which was called the White River, had nothing but mud and a few water holes sometimes. Evan hoped it would not go completely dry. If it did he would have no way to water the cattle.

On a hot July day, Evan returned to the house for dinner. He and

Dub had been raking and stacking hay for the winter. As he entered Mary said, "Evan you look hot and tired. Remember you had a heart attack not so very long ago. Sit out on the porch and rest while I finish fixing dinner."

"I'm fine. You don't need to worry about me."

"I didn't say I was worried. I just said you should rest from time to time. We got a letter from Milla you must read." Mary smiled.

"Bet I can guess why you are smiling. Milla is going to have a baby, right."

"Oh, sit down and read the letter, smarty."

Evan read the letter then said, "Well, Babe, you are going to be a grandmother for the third time, maybe I should quit calling you, Babe."

"Evan, you are the grandparent, remember? I'm the hired girl."

"Yeah, I know. I always said I had to try you out before I married you."

"EVAN!! Don't you ever say that again! I would be so embarrassed."

"Now don't go getting mad. I have never said that to anyone else. I was just teasing you."

"Maybe so, but I know you, Evan Furman, you might say that. Then what do I say?"

"Just say you knew what a catch I would be so you married me."

"Oh, you are going through a second childhood."

"Well if I am, it's more fun the second time."

Dub came in the house just then. Mary shook her head and said, "Dinner is on the table. Dub if you have already washed up, we'll eat." Dub looked at both of them and could tell there was some joke between them, but didn't ask."

CHAPTER 13

Whatever your hand finds to do, do it with all your might

In September 1936 Milla delivered a baby girl. Milla had no problems during the delivery. Larry was so full of pride he handed out cigars to everyone he saw whether he knew them or not.

Evan and Mary didn't have a telephone yet but Ruth did, so Larry called her to announce the news. He then asked if she would drive out and tell Evan and Mary. Ruth had taken a job with REA in South Dakota and was living in Martin, with her husband, Roy. She was pleased to be a part of spreading the family news. Two weeks later, Evan and Mary drove to Rushville to see their granddaughter.

"What's her name?" Evan asked.

Milla answered, "Kathleen Fay."

Mary said, "That's a pretty name and she is such a pretty baby."

Evan added, "Of course she is. I wouldn't expect anything but a pretty granddaughter."

Milla said, "So you think she looks like me?"

Evan laughed, "Certainly!"

Larry said, "You two are just alike."

As Christmas approached that year, Evan said to Mary, "Babe, it has been a long time since either one of us bought anything or had any new clothes. When was the last time?"

"I don't keep track of that sort of thing." After a pause Mary continued, "I did get a new dress a couple of years ago and I seem to remember your buying bib overalls some time back. We really don't need anything, so why are you bringing this up?"

"I was just thinking it would be nice to have something new."

"Evan, what have you got on your mind?"

"You know me pretty well, don't you?"

"I should, considering everything we have been through in the 21 years we have been married. So what do you want to buy?"

"I thought it would be good to have a radio so we would know what is going on in the rest of the world."

"A radio, I have never given a thought to having a radio. It sounds like a luxury thing to me. Besides, we can't change a thing good or bad that happens so why do we need to know what is going on in the world."

"I just think it would be nice to hear of things when they happen, not 2 months later from someone who heard or read about it. There other are things on the radio beside news. There is music and entertainment."

"You have your mind made up, don't you?"

Evan sheepishly answered, "Well, sort of. I'm not sure what a radio would cost and I must admit it is not something we need to have. But I think we could find a little money for one."

"If you can pay for one, buy it and we will consider it a Christmas present to each other. I might listen to it while I am cooking or ironing."

The next time Evan was in Martin he bought a crystal operating radio. He felt like a young boy with a new toy. That night he listened to KMOX in Yankton, South Dakota. Mary and Dub sat by the radio and listened as well. The radio made them feel like they were a part of something bigger than three people on the South Dakota prairie. Now they did not feel isolated from the rest of the world.

One evening, Evan said to Mary and Dub, "I feel like I know much more now about what is happening everywhere and can discuss things more intelligently. This radio is an educational tool as well as an entertainment source"

Mary looked over at Evan and said, "True, but it has changed the way we do things. I'm not sure that is good."

Dub asked, "How has the radio changed us?"

"Look how we stay up later than we used to and how we seem to rush through evening chores and supper just to sit down and listen to the radio."

"You're right Babe but I don't think that hurts anything."

The radio changed their lives in many ways. Not only did they hear up-to-date news, Evan could keep abreast of current grain and cattle prices. It provided entertainment as well. There were programs of humor and music. Dub thought those programs were the best. Mary listened some during the day but would say, "It's just a lot of noise in my opinion." They soon realized that batteries lasted longer the less the radio was played. So radio usage became sparser.

On very cold snowy days that winter the radio use increased and remained at a higher level until the batteries died. Then it would not be used again until the roads were clear enough to drive to Martin and cash was available to buy more batteries.

There were a lot of cold days that February. The temperatures were below zero more than above. Getting hay to the cattle and breaking the ice in the creek bed so the cattle could drink was a struggle.

On the days when it was too cold to work outside, Evan spent much of his time playing solitaire on his old wooden desk. He would turn the radio on at noon to hear the market reports, and again in the evening for the 6 o'clock news. He only went out for the most necessary chores. He felt caged up on these days. Solitaire helped him concentrate on other things.

The spring of 1937 brought a return of dust storms. Evan planted oats as soon as the ground was warm enough to allow seed to germinate. In late May a dust storm started and lasted for 48 hours. Evan worried dust would blow into the cattle's noses. If that happened, they could suffocate. They were in open country where only a few trees offered any cover. Fortunately, nature had educated animals to turn their rear ends into the wind during blizzards and dust storms.

He was also concerned about the tender oat plants that were less than 4 inches high. The field of oats was on a level plateau east of the house. The wind could be very strong blowing across that field. The tender plants could be covered up or blown right out of the ground.

When the storm first started, the three of them had just sat down for their noon meal. When the wind began Evan said, "Dub, it looks like a bad one coming. We better try to close up the brooder houses before it gets any worse."

Evan and Dub immediately went out. They struggled through the wind and dust to close the doors on the buildings for the chickens and turkeys. Evan knew that some of them had the sense to go to shelter, but not all. Those that were not inside some shelter might not survive. The blowing dust was so thick there was no point in trying to find any of them. They could still see but finding their way back to the house would not be an easy task for the two men.

They had just gotten inside the door when the full fury of the storm hit.

Mary was doing what she could to cover windows and doors with blankets, towels or anything she could find to stuff into cracks. She could hear the sand coming down the inside of the stovepipe to the cook stove. There was nothing she could do to stop that. She had been making a rug from rags. She used it to cover the cabinets containing flour and sugar.

Around five in the afternoon of the second day, the wind stopped and the sun could be seen. The cleanup began. First in the house, Evan and Dub used brooms and shovels to remove the worst of the sand. Mary shook out the blankets and towels used over the windows and doors. Next she wiped off all the furniture. After that all the dishes and pans would be washed. "Thank goodness the flour and sugar was protected by the rag rugs." Mary said aloud.

While she was doing that, Evan and Dub started shoveling sand out of the chicken and turkey houses. Then the barn had to be shoveled out. It was late that night before they stopped to eat something.

Evan said, "Dub, early tomorrow, you ride across the creek and see how the cattle made out. I'll finish up the barn and help your Mother here in the house."

"Evan, you take care of the animals and the barn. Then why don't you drive over and see if Jim and Helen made it through alright. I can handle the clean-up on the inside."

After Evan had done all he could to remove the sand from the barn, he drove down to see Jim and Helen. There were some places in the roadway where dirt and sand was piled up like drifted snow.

Evan would speed up and hit them head-on. He never got stuck, but dirt and sand would fly out like spraying water whenever he plowed through one. When he got to Jim's place, Helen was sweeping dirt out the front door of their house. Evan could tell she had been crying. She greeted him and asked, "Is Mary alright?" She gave no hint as to why she had been crying.

"She's fine.", then Evan surprised her by saying, "Helen, I know you never experienced a dust storm back east, but neither had we until a few years ago. There will be some good times. You must always think that."

"No, I've never seen anything like these dust storms and I've never seen a blizzard until I moved out here. I try to be positive, but it is very hard for me to do so."

"Think about your fine boys and the funny things they do or think about how refreshing the air is after a rain. Think of anything that will make you smile."

"I do try. It's just all this sand and dirt. Please don't tell Jim you found me crying. He is cleaning out the barn."

"I won't tell. How bad is the inside of your house?"

"I have cleaned the worst out. Now I need to wash everything and I mean everything."

"I know; Mary is doing the same. I'll go out to the barn and talk to Jim."

Jim greeted Evan, "I'm surprised to see you. I thought you would be digging out of this mess too. Did the storm miss you?"

"No, we got hit just like you did. Dub is out now checking on the cattle and there is still more cleaning up to do. I wanted to see if you and Helen were alright."

"I guess we are the same as everyone else. We didn't lose any cows; that's the good part. As for the wheat, I doubt if we can harvest a crop this fall. There is not enough wheat sprouts left in the field to fill a sack. Maybe we can use what is left for seed next year."

"Where are the boys? I want to see them."

"Mike is around here somewhere and Bill is up at the house with Helen." Jim called loudly, "Mike."

A head raised up in the hayloft. "You want me, Dad?"

"Grandpa is here; he wants to see you."

"Hi, Grandpa."

Evan asked, "Are you hiding from the bad guys?"

"Naw, I just got up here to get out of all the sand that is everywhere."

"Why don't you go help your Mother? She could use your help."

"Grandpa is right. You need to help your Mother clean up."

"Ok." Mike climbed down and ran to the house.

Evan turned toward Jim, "Glad you didn't lose any livestock. Sorry about your wheat. When I get home, I'm going to check on how our oats made out. They may be worthless too. Everyone is in the same shape. The only good thing is grain prices will be high because of the crop shortages."

"That will be good only if you have anything to sell."

Say, why don't you and Helen and the boys come over for dinner this Sunday?"

"Sounds good to me and I'm sure Helen would appreciate it."

"Jim, you might try planting some corn. It's not too late to do that. With some rain this summer you could get a decent yield."

"I'm not sure corn would grow in this sandy soil, plus I don't have the money to buy seed."

As Evan returned home he thought, "Those two need to have something good happen. Maybe Babe has an idea as to how we could help them."

He drove past the house up to the plateau where the oats had been planted. After he turned into the field, he could see there was no point in even getting out of the car. He looked across the field and said aloud, "I can count on one hand the plants left. I guess I might as well follow my advice to Jim and plant corn." Both Evan and Jim replaced their lost crops with corn. Evan bought the seed.

During the summer Evan and Mary received a letter from Milla informing them that she was expecting another baby sometime in late October. Since Mary usually got the mail first, she told Evan when he came in that evening. "Our family is growing. We got a letter from Milla saying you will get your fourth grandchild in October."

"That's great. I look forward to having more little ones around again. I hope they visit a lot."

"You missed spending time with your own children when you were in the automobile business. Now you will get another chance with grandchildren."

"You are right, Babe. Looking back, I can see that now but at the time I thought making a good life for my family required a lot of working hours. You should have told me that I should be spending more time with the kids."

"Would you have listened to me if I had told you?"

"Probably not then, but I would now. Thanks to you, the kids turned out great."

Fall came and the corn yield did about average for the area. However, the price for corn dropped dramatically because all the farmers replanted using corn. On the other hand, wheat and oat prices went up. Both Evan and Jim harvested their corn crop, and wondered if it was worth the effort since they would receive very little money. Both decided there was no point in selling their corn crop. Instead, they would use it for cattle feed.

Milla's baby arrived the third week in October. They named him Lawrence Ellis, after his father. As the boy grew, he was given the nickname, Pete, since most everyone called his father Larry. His father was so proud of his newborn son that he not only passed out cigars; he bought a round of drinks at the Rushville saloon. Afterward Milla asked, "What were you thinking about? We don't have the money to be buying drinks for everyone in town."

"Guess I got carried away. But it's not every day a man gets a son. I just had to do something."

"Well next time, do something that doesn't cost so much." It would not be until 15 years later that Milla would have another child. She would give birth to a daughter that lived only one day. Fate seemed unkind to Milla because the day she was born, her mother died. Now her second daughter would only live one day. Milla wondered why death and birth seemed to be attached to her.

During 1937 Evan, Mary and Dub lived from day to day. Money was almost nonexistent in the Furman household. Jim and his family were in the same condition. Evan said to Mary, "Babe, once again your garden is saving us from starving. Thank God it was plentiful enough to feed Jim's family too"

"It has been a Godsend. Jim and Helen have worked in the garden as much as I have. That is why it could provide for two families."

The economy did not get any better but it did not get worse either. The weather was favorable. There were rains in the spring which stimulated plant growth and in turn provided a good crop yield. However every farmer got a good yield so there was a surplus of grain being sold. This resulted in a lower price in the market. The cash Evan received was less than he thought he would receive for his wheat. Still it was cash in his pocket.

After the wheat was sold, Evan, Jim, and Dub discussed their plight.

Dub said, "I wonder if we will ever be any better off. The larger the yield we get, the less the price for grain; and when we get a small yield there is not enough wheat to provide much cash. What's the use?"

"That's the way the market works; supply and demand. The big processors are the only ones who seem to gain anything. The small farmer doesn't stand a chance." added Jim.

"Boys, it's like I heard someone say, "Don't kick a fresh cow pie in the summertime."

Jim asked, "What do you mean by that?"

"You two are talking like someone crapped all over you. Well, they didn't. We should be thankful it isn't any worse. So don't complain about what we can't control."

"Dad, we know we can't do anything about prices but we don't like it and want it known we don't like what's going on."

As they left the co-op, Evan thought, "Now that I have a little money, what could I buy Mary that would help her? She does what she can to bring in some money. She should get some benefit for her efforts." Then he remembered she was heating the flat irons to iron clothes as he left the house this morning. "That's it, a gas-fired iron!" he said aloud. He went to Gambles and purchased a gas iron.

He had a big grin on his face when he walked into the house. "What have you done now, Evan?"

"Babe, I've got something for you."

"What?"

"Guess."

"Knowing you, it's hard to say."

"How about a gas iron so you don't have to heat flat irons on the stove any longer?"

"Evan, that is thoughtful of you. It will make ironing easier, but I really never minded using the flat irons."

Daily routines in life continued as it always had. On Tuesdays, Evan would fill the butter churn with milk after the morning milking. He would crank the handle until butter began to form. When it became firm enough, he would take it out of the churn and put it in a wooden bowl.

Mary then took over. She worked the moisture out with a wooden paddle. Then she pressed the butter into a wooden box until it was solid. When she was satisfied that it was solid enough, she pushed it out of the box and wrapped it in wax paper. It would be stored in the ice box until it was used up. Ice was delivered on Wednesdays if a request was made by noon on Tuesdays. Going into town every week did not occur; hence, no one might be in town on Tuesday. On those weeks there would be no ice in the icebox. Their only option to deal with the lack of ice was to store food in the "cellar". The cellar was dug into a hillside with a heavy door over the mouth of it. There were stairs going down inside. The temperature normally was 50to 60 degrees.

The churn was left containing buttermilk, which Evan loved. He would pour himself a glass of buttermilk, and then pour the remainder into a pitcher for Mary to use in making pancakes.

Mary made chokecherry jelly, as always, and picked strawberries which were sold in town. When garden produce was plentiful she would sell that as well. Eggs were usually traded at the grocery store for flour, sugar or canned goods. She did everything she could think of to add to the family income.

The winter of 1937 was cold and snowy. Evan and all of his children's families experienced a scarcity of cash. Jim and Helen suffered the most. Jim even burned ears of corn for fuel to heat their home. He had no money for coal or wood. Evan worried about all his children but felt hopeless because he could not help. He and Mary shared food that Mary had canned from their garden with Jim and Helen. When they went to town they always took something to Ruth.

Milla and Larry received food that Mary had canned when they came to visit. Usually everybody that visited went home with a chicken or possibly a turkey as well as the canned food.

Everyone felt blessed that there were no blizzards that winter even though there were more snowfalls than normal. When spring came in 1938, hope came with it. Rains came and the hills were as green as any hills in Ireland.

When the frozen ground thawed, Evan and Jim planted corn and wheat. They both felt optimistic that there was going to be a bumper crop which would result in a good income.

On the Fourth of July, Bob and Park Shelby, their closest neighbor, came over for a noon meal. No work would be done because this was a holiday that should be celebrated. The fourth of July was unlike the winter holidays when travel and outdoor activities were restricted. The weather in summer was more cooperative than the winter for get togethers.

So it made sense for gatherings to happen on the 4th of July.

The table on the porch was moved to the center and was covered with a white tablecloth. There was fried chicken, a beef roast, all kinds of vegetables, and three kinds of pie for dessert. When everyone had eaten more than they should, Evan said, "Why don't we move out under the trees in the front yard, it would be cooler?"

The women cleared the table and washed the dishes. Bob and Evan took chairs out for their wives, but both of them and Dub sat on the ground leaning against a tree. The men talked about the price for cattle and wheat. Then their conversation turned to what they heard about the war in Europe.

As the women came out of the house, Park asked Mary, "What are your children and their families doing today?"

"Milla and Larry invited Jim and his family over to their house. Ruth and her husband are with some of their neighbors and I'm not sure what Jessie is doing."

About six o'clock, Bob said, "Mother, we had better head home. I've got a cow to milk."

"Where has the time gone? I'll get my dishes and be ready."

Mary said, "Take some of the chicken and that pie that we didn't cut home with you."

The two families getting together on the Fourth of July would be an annual event for years to come.

Later that summer a hail storm hit the area. The wheat and the corn were shredded. As soon as it ended, Evan walked across the road and looked over the field where the wheat had been planted. He told Dub, "I don't think there is anything left to harvest. About all we can do is turn the cattle out in the field and let them glean what they can. I hope Jim did not get hit this badly."

Dub said, "Do you think we will ever get two good years in a row?"

"Dub, we just have to take what God gives us and do the best we can."

Jim's fields were damaged, but not as bad as Evan's fields. So Jim was able to harvest enough wheat to sell. But his yield was low, hence the income was not what he had hoped for.

Fall meant it was time to bring in the steers going to the market. Evan had only sold steers since he began farming five years ago. He kept all heifer calves. His herd had expanded to the point of needing more land.

Jim had sold only steers as well; usually in conjunction with Evan. His herd still only numbered 20 breed cows and a borrowed bull from his uncle Leo.

CHAPTER 14

Since no man knows the future, who can tell him what is to come?

January 17, 1939 Evan's mother, Belle, died. Evan and Mary made preparations to go to Rushville. Remembering the trip to James' funeral, Evan said, "Death never comes at a convenient time. Maybe that is God's way of testing our feelings toward the departed one."

"I don't know if you are right or not Evan, but I will miss Belle. She was always good to me"

The weather was cold but there was no snow to contend with on the trip. After the funeral, the family gathered for a meal at the family ranch. When they finished eating, the heirs started discussing what to do about the ranch. J.B. and the sisters felt the ranch should be divided equally among those still alive. There was no agreement on who should get what area. Everyone seemed to have some strong opinions. Evan and Leo were silent.

J. B., noticing Evan's silence, asked, "Evan, you have not said any thing. What section do you want?"

"I wondered if anyone was interested in what I thought. Now I'm going to tell you all how it is going to be. Leo took care of our parents until they died. He stayed on the ranch and even built it up more; we all left. When we did, we gave up ours rights to anything. He deserves the ranch; we don't. I say Leo gets everything. He should be the rightful owner now. And I'll shoot anyone that doesn't agree and tries to cause a problem."

No one said anything. None of them wanted to buck Evan. They all wondered if Evan really would shoot anyone who disagreed. Much later Mary was asked if she thought Evan would shoot J B or a sister if they went against him. Mary answered, "Yes, I think he would have." The homestead place stayed intact and under the control of one person. Leo would be forever grateful to Evan

In the spring the stories of war in Europe were the main topics of conversation. Hitler's armies invaded Poland, then rolled over Denmark, Belgium, and into France. Many Americans wanted nothing to do with the war in Europe. They favored an isolationist policy. This was congress' attitude as well.

Meanwhile, in America the economy began to improve and the dust storms were fewer. Grain prices did not fall and the value of beef cattle rose. There was hope in Evan's thinking again. He had money to carry in his pocket again.

"Mary, I think the bad times are about over. At least I hope so. The way it looks now, I will be able to buy a new hay rake this fall. We sure need one."

One sign of an improved economy was a telephone line being installed beside the road in front of their house. "Mary, I think we could afford to hook into the telephone line. What would you think about having a telephone?"

"I think that would be great. We could talk to the kids once in awhile."

Evan enjoyed having Jim and his family close by. He encouraged Jim's boys to visit and to stay overnight. Mike and Bill thought going to Grandpa and Grandma's was a real treat. As soon as the boys walked into the house, Mike would say, "Grandma, you got any cinnamon rolls?" Evan would laugh and say, "Is that why you came to visit?" Grandma always made cinnamon rolls and to the boys they were better than candy, which they very rarely received.

After enjoying the rolls, the next thing the boys would ask, "Grandpa, can we ride Old Blue?" Old Blue was a gentle workhorse that Evan had kept mostly for the boys to ride, but was still useful when there were cattle to move. Evan would always answer yes. The boys would follow Evan out to the calf pasture where Blue was kept. Evan would put a bridle on Blue and hand the reins to Mike. Bill would say, "Why does Mike always get to lead Blue?

Evan would pick Bill up and say, "Because he is the oldest. Some day it will be your turn."

Mike would lead Blue over to the side of the basement house and then climb on the roof, from which he could mount the horse. Evan would lift Bill up behind Mike. Bill would sit there but ask, "When can I get on the horse like Mike?"

"When you are big enough to get on the basement house roof like your brother." Evan explained to him.

Bill spent the rest of the summer trying to climb on the basement house roof. Finally, in early September, by standing first on a wooden box, Bill managed to climb onto the basement house roof. He had conquered his mountain.

He went to find Evan. When he could not find his Grandpa, He went in the house and ask, "Grandma where is Grandpa?"

"I think he is out checking on cattle and fences." Bill wanted to go out to look for him but Mary told him no. Disappointed, Bill went back out, shaded his eyes and looked in all directions. There was no sign of his Grandpa. He thought if he climbed back on the roof of the basement house he could see farther. Bill waited; finally, he saw Evan coming back. Full of energy and success, he jumped down and ran to the edge of the barnyard. As soon as Evan got close, he waved and yelled out, "Grandpa, I can climb on the roof now! Come watch and I'll show you."

Evan rode his horse over to the basement house and watched as Bill displayed his new skills. "Well, looks like you are ready to mount old Blue like your brother." Bill felt like he had just climbed Mount Everest.

Throwing his arms into the air Bill yelled, "Yea!". Then as he jumped down, he tumbled forward onto his face. Evan chuckled but offered no help. "You don't need to get too big for your britches, young fellow."

"Yes Grandpa, can I go tell Grandma that I get to ride Blue?"

"Go tell her."

From then on, when the boys would ride Old Blue, Mike would climb on the basement house roof then pull Bill up after him. From there, Mike would jump up and worm his way onto Blue's back, then pull Bill up. A couple of times the process didn't work and the two boys would fall back onto the roof. When that happened, Old Blue would just stand still. He would turn his head as if giving the boys a smile and wait for the two to try again.

When they were successful, the two would ride all around the open space between the road, house and barn. Evan would not allow them to venture away from the house. Mike would try to coax Old Blue into a trot but Blue sensed she should be careful with young boys on her back.

Evan had another animal which kept Bill in line. That was a dog named Shep. When Mike would get to leave the house with Evan, and Bill was left behind, Bill would try to follow. Shep would get in front of Bill and stand. Bill would try to walk around him, without success. Wherever Bill moved, Shep moved. No matter what Bill did, Shep stood in front of Bill and kept him near the house. Finally Bill would give up and hunt for something else to occupy his time.

Unfortunately, a blizzard came without any warning in January, 1940. Evan had moved his cattle into the trees along the creek just for this reason. The trees would provide some protection from wind and blowing snow.

Jim's cattle were on the open range without any shelter. After the snow stopped falling, there was 16 inches of snow on the ground and the temperature stayed below zero for a week. When Jim finally got to them, they were all dead. He could not believe what he saw. Their bodies lay in a small circle. They had huddled together for warmth and protection from the snow but could not survive the long cold period without food and water.

He got off his horse, dropped to his knees in the snow and cried out, "Noooo." Jim stared at the dead carcasses that were to be his future. A half hour later the horse nudged him. He became aware of the cold and that his pant legs were wet. He stood up, took one more look at the carnage, and then mounted his horse. As he rode back to the house, he felt broken and lost. His guts had just been ripped out of him. He had to tell Helen, but what would he tell her?

Jim walked into the house stoned faced and blurted out, "All our cattle are dead. What do we do now?"

Helen had just put more corncobs and wood in the stove. She turned to Jim, "What are you saying?"

"I'm saying everything is lost. We have no cattle. We are broke. We harvested such a small crop of wheat last fall. And what money we got from that, is gone. With all the cattle dead, we have no way to get any money this year. We can't pay the interest on the mortgage." Jim's face was ash colored and his eyes had a look of despair.

There was silence in the room. Helen searched for the right words. "Jim, even though you have tried your best, nothing seems to be working. Maybe it is time we do something else. My Mother's last letter said there were jobs available back in Indiana. Let's move back there. I think you could find some kind of work. There are many businesses back east and some of them must be looking for workers. We can make a life there."

"Move to Indiana; that sounds drastic."

"Jim, you just said we have no money and there are no jobs out here. That is why we left Gordon. What other choice do we have?"

"I don't know what to do. And I'll admit there are no jobs here. Let's go talk to my Dad. Maybe he can suggest something."

With a heavy heart, Jim and Helen put their two boys in the old pickup and drove to Evan's house. When they got there, Evan could tell by the look on Jim's face that something was wrong.

"Looks like you two were rode hard and put away wet. What's wrong?"

Jim answered, "All our cattle are dead. The blizzard did them in. On top of that, last fall's wheat crop was so small that we didn't get much cash. And now we have no money. We can't make the spring mortgage payment so the bank will foreclose. We have nothing and soon we will have no place to live."

Nobody said anything until Bill asked, "Grandma, you got any cinnamon rolls?"

"Sure, I've some that just came out of the oven. Why don't you boys come with me into the kitchen for some warm cinnamon rolls." Evan said, "Son, you still have your family and your health. That's something to be thankful for. You'll just have to start building again. It's been done before. If you can't pay the mortgage, you and Helen can move back into the basement house."

"Dad, I'm not sure I want to start over. I can't help but feel God is telling me that I wasn't supposed to be a farmer. Maybe I should be working for some company someplace. But where do I go to find some kind of job around here?"

"I'm doubtful you could find work around here. And Jim, I

know your feeling. I felt the same way when the automobile business collapsed"

Jim said, "Helen's mother says there are jobs available in Indiana and I know Helen would like to move back there. If we did and I found a job, then I could at least feed my family. But to do that seems like I am giving up and leaving everything I've ever known. I don't like that thought either."

"Jim, this is a decision you have to make. I would hate to see you and your family move. But as I told you once before, there are no promises in this life."

"I know that Dad; I just don't know what to decide. I want to stay around here but I can't feed my family here."

"You are right; a move to Indiana will take you away from everything you have ever known. But your thinking is also right about providing for your family. You have a wife and you brought two boys into this world; you are responsible for them. You must think about their welfare first regardless of what you want."

"I know. I just don't want to do what seems obvious."

Evan wanted to put his arms around Jim but didn't. "I can't say what's right for you and your family. Only you can make that decision. Whatever you decide, you must live with it. All I can say is try to think about where it makes the most sense for you to provide for your family."

There was silence. Then Evan said, "Why don't the four of you stay with us tonight and we'll talk some more about it tomorrow."

Before Jim could answer, Helen said, "Let's stay, Jim."

That night after everyone had gone to bed, Evan said to Mary, "How I hate the thought of Jim and his family being 1,000 miles away. I know it is a selfish thought. Jim needs an income. That is what is important. I just keep asking myself; if they move to Indiana, when would we ever see them?'

"I agree, Evan, but Jim can't find work here and he feels like it is not meant for him to be a farmer or rancher. Moving east may be the right thing for him to do. If it is, we can't encourage him to stay here."

"True. But I will sure miss those boys."

"Someday, times will be better and we can visit them. Or the boys could come out here for the summer."

"We will have to wait and see but I hope so."

"Evan, you know they don't have the money to move."

"Yes, I know."

Mary said, "Would you object to our giving them the money? I know it would take all the cash we have."

"Bless you, Babe, for suggesting that. I was not going to say anything. We can get by without any cash. We have before and some day we may need to do so again. If they decide to move, we can offer to give them the money for train tickets."

Jim and Helen also had a discussion. Jim said, "I'm not sure I can leave my family and this country. It's all I've ever known."

Helen said, "Jim, you will miss them but it gets easier with time. When I came out here it took me a while to get over missing my family." Neither Jim nor Helen said anything for several minutes. Then Helen continued, "Jim, there just doesn't seem to be a way for you maintain an income out here. You could find some type of work in Indiana, I'm sure. The boys and I will be with you. You will have that much of your family."

"Remember, we don't have any money. Where could we live?"

"I know we could stay with my parents until you found a job."

"I suppose so, but I don't like having other people provide for my family. The thought of that makes me feel guilty. And besides, your parents never have met me. How are they going to feel about someone they never met living in their house?"

"They'll welcome you with open arms. Jim, we lived with your parents. You didn't say anything then. What other option do we have?"

"I suppose you're right there." Jim stared at the ceiling then he asked, "If we move back east, where are we going to get the money to move?"

Helen answered, "I could write to my parents. I know they would help."

"I don't want to start imposing on your parents before we even get there."

"Are you saying we will move back to Indiana?"

"I guess I am. I don't know what else to do."

There was no more conversation. The room was dark and quiet, yet sleep was not granted to any adult that night.

The next morning, after they had eaten a breakfast of bacon, eggs and pancakes, Mary and Helen cleared the table and washed the dishes. The two men remained at the table saying nothing. Finally Evan broke the silence by saying, "Jim, if you decide to go to Indiana, we'll pay for your train tickets."

"We have decided to go." After a pause he continued, "I appreciate your offer and it is very kind. I don't know when I could repay you."

"Don't concern yourself about it. We all need help at one time or another in our lives. And families help their family when troubles come."

Two weeks later, after Jim and Helen had given most of what furniture they had to Jim's sisters, it was time to go. It was a cold winter day when Evan and Mary drove Jim and his family to the train station in Merriman, Nebraska. Evan fought back tears. Mary, Jim and Helen were not as successful. It was a sad parting. There were hugs and wishes for better times but no dry eyes. The boys, not realizing the situation, only felt excitement about a train ride. They boarded the train and found a seat by the window. Evan and Mary waved goodbye as the train pulled away. The boys and Helen waved back. Jim closed his eyes and wondered what life was going to be like.

Evan said nothing all the way back to their house. The empty feeling inside of him would stay for a long time. Mary knew his feelings. "Evan, when summer comes why don't we invite Milla's two children to spend a few days with us?"

"That sounds like a good idea, Babe."

Three weeks went by before a letter arrived from Jim and Helen. All it said was that they had made the trip without any problems. The boys thought it had been a great adventure. They were staying with Helen's parents. There was little else written. Evan hoped there was not a problem.

Mary said, "Evan, don't try to read between the lines. Jim and Helen are just getting adjusted to a different place. When Jim finds a job and they get a house to live in, I'm sure they will be fine."

In June, Milla and her two children arrived one Sunday about noon. Evan suggested they stay for a few days.

"Dad, we can't do that. I didn't bring any clothes for us to stay."

Mary said, "Well, stay the night anyway. I'll wash out anything you need after the children are in bed."

"Larry said you would want us to stay. I should have brought some clothes for the kids. I was smart enough to bring extra underwear for Pete just in case. I think it would be alright to stay one night."

Evan began telling Kathleen and Pete about his school days. Kathleen sat and listened, taking in every word. Pete was more interested in his toy truck. Mary guided Milla into the kitchen where Evan could not hear and said, "Milla, would you consider letting Kathleen and Pete come back for a week or two? That would mean a great deal to your dad."

"Mom, Kathleen would be alright if she doesn't get home sick. Pete is so young, I'm not sure about him."

"Milla, your Dad misses Jim's two boys in the worst way and he thinks your two are something special. If you would let your children come for a visit, it would be an immense help to him."

"Let me talk to Larry. If he doesn't think Pete is too young, then we'll bring them over for a short stay." Larry felt Pete was old enough to be away from his mother for a week. "Let the kids go for a week since your parents want them to come for a visit. Besides, it will give us some time to ourselves."

Milla said, "I don't know, Larry. Pete is so young and my parents are not used to young children."

"They will get along just fine, and the kids will love it."

"Alright, we'll try it. I'll take them over next Saturday." Thus started an annual ritual of one or both spending part of the summer with Evan and Mary.

A letter finally came from Jim.

Dear Folks,

This sure is a different country. There are a lot more trees and people here. Also city living is different than living in Gordon. We found a house to rent and are living in Indianapolis where I'm employed. I have been employed by a dairy company to deliver milk and dairy products to homes.

The boys have adjusted well and they have neighborhood playmates that keep them busy. Helen is pleased because there is a library only a block away. She gets books to read all the time. We are all doing fine.

Your Son,
Jim

Evan and Mary felt less concern after reading the letter. "Sounds like they are beginning to settle into a new way of life," Evan told Mary.

Later that evening the phone rang; Mary answered. "It's Milla. She said she would bring Kathleen and little Pete over to stay for three or four days."

"Good. Believe it or not, I still haven't gotten used to that phone ringing. I guess I will someday. Say, it's been a long time since we have had little ones around. What will we do to keep them occupied?"

"What do you mean – we? You'll be out of the house most of the day."

"There's not that much going on right now. Dub can take care of most of it."

"Evan, I'll give you one day, and then you'll find some excuse to be outside except when it is time to eat."

"When I go out, I'll take the little ones with me."

"You can't do that. They are too little. It will be another three or four years before they will be old enough to spend very much time out in a field someplace."

"I wasn't talking about that sort of thing. I was just thinking about going to the barn or the granary."

"You better just think about taking them out to the front yard."

"We'll see."

Kathleen and Pete's visit was a joyful one. But after three days, they were ready to see their Mom. Evan and Mary drove them back to their Rushville home.

As the two of them returned toward Martin, Mary said, "I had forgotten how much energy little ones have. I am ready for a day of rest."

During their annual Fourth of July get together, Bob Shelby said to Evan, "Do you think we'll be dragged into the war in Europe?"

"Who knows? My guess is, it will get worse. Hitler seems to want to control the entire world."

"Sounds like you feel we will be involved before long."

"I hope not. There were a lot of good men killed the last time we went to Europe to fight. I don't want to see that happen again."

"But you just said you thought it would get worse."

"That's the way it looks. Hitler has captured all of France and most of Europe."

"I read about the Germans trapping the British and French armies at Dunkirk. And the English sent every small boat in the country over to evacuate the soldiers. That was sure something."

"Yes, it was. Churchill said it was a miracle. Now England is being bombed and may be attacked. If they fall, we'll be next. I think that is why Roosevelt got congress to pay for some new ships and provide more defense money."

Bob said, "I wonder if Roosevelt is the warmonger that Wendell Willkie says he is. He just might beat Roosevelt. What do you think?"

"I don't think Roosevelt is a warmonger, but I will vote for Willkie. Because I agree with him about the way Roosevelt has handled the economy. There are still as many men without a job as ever."

Mary approached the two men and said, "Could you two stop solving the world's problems long enough to eat?"

Evan laughed, "Well, Bob, I think we have some important work to do."

"I agree. The world will just have to get along without us for a while."

The two men went inside, washed their hands and sat down at a table full of food. When everyone finished what was on their plates, Mary noticed Evan's eyes looking around. She let him look for a minute, and then got up from the table, "Yes, Evan there is pie for dessert."

Evan had a sheepish look on his face, but that didn't stop him from announcing, "Pie is the only true dessert. I told our kids dessert is spelled P-I-E."

Summer turned to fall. Evan and Dub separated the steers from the herd and drove them to a small pasture near the barn. Two days before the fall auction, Evan and Dub loaded the steers into a truck, borrowed from Leo, and drove them to the auction.

Buyers from the east attended the auctions. Many friendships developed between the buyers and the western stock men. Cattle auctions were one of the highlights of the year. Wives went with their husbands and socialized while the bidding took placed. In the evening a dance was held and well attended. Mary was not as much of a dancer as Evan, but she attended as well, mostly to please Evan.

Early in November, Evan said to Dub, "Let's move the cattle from the north range down to the creek. I don't want them to get caught in the open if there is a snow storm. Besides the grass is about gone where they are."

Dub replied, "That will sure make it easier to feed them this winter. We may need to check the fences first. I noticed a broken fencepost on the south side of the creek."

"Guess I have missed seeing that. Tomorrow, let's replace that post and repair anything that looks weak. I would like to get the cattle moved before the end of the week."

When Thanksgiving time came around, Evan said to Mary, "Wouldn't it be great if Jim and Helen brought the boys out for Thanksgiving."

"Now, Evan, you know that is not going to happen. It would take them three days to get here besides the cost involved. We will have Milla and her family here if it doesn't snow too much."

"I know, but Jim and his family has been on my mind. I miss them, but having Milla's family here will be good. Are we going to have turkey?"

"Don't we always have turkey for Thanksgiving? Well, for the last three years anyway. Before that we didn't raise turkeys did we?"

"No, and I remember a couple of years where we just had potatoes, beans and carrots."

"I'm glad things are a little better now."

The day after Thanksgiving a letter arrived from Helen. It read:

> ***Dear Folks,***
>
> ***I am sorry to tell you Jim and I have divorced. It is probably as much my fault as his. But what is done is done, so who's at fault is not going to change anything. I just wanted you both to know how much I always thought of you and still do. You were always great and loving to me and I appreciated that.***
>
> ***The boys will never hear anything but good words about their grandparents in South Dakota. I hope some day they can visit the two of you.***
>
> ***Sincerely***
> ***Helen***

Mary spoke first, "How sad. I thought things would work out when they moved to Indiana. Their marriage seemed to be strong when they left here. What do you think happened?"

"I don't know what happened, but it has. It's too late to go back now. If they had stayed out here, could we have prevented it from happening? Maybe; we'll never know. I just feel terrible because they have divorced. Kids need both a father and a mother. I still remember how hard it was before we were married and I was trying to take care of four little ones."

"At least Helen has good feelings about us. I am thankful for that. I always thought very highly of her. It was good that she did express willingness for the boys to come for a visit, so maybe that can be done someday."

"I'm grateful for that too but I don't know how to make that happen. We'll just wait and see what can be done about Mike and Bill coming for a visit."

"Evan, the only way they could come is by train and they are too young to make a trip like that without someone being with them."

"I know that and I also realize neither Jim nor Helen have the money for train tickets. Damn the 1,000 miles between us."

"Evan don't lose your temper."

"I'm not losing my temper. I just would like for things to be different. I'm glad Milla's two live close enough to visit. They are two good kids."

"Maybe next summer Kathleen and Pete could take the train from Rushville to Merriman. That is not as far as a trip from Indiana and they would not need to change trains any place. We could meet them there and make sure they got off at the right place."

"Sounds like a good idea to me."

The year of 1941 began with reasonable weather and the price for steers was favorable. The war news in Europe seemed far away. Wheat was planted and the spring rains signaled a good yield for the fall harvest. Evan felt better than he had for the last four years. He improved even more when Kathleen and Pete came for their annual visit in June.

Evan placed a cot by the north window of the living room for the two to sleep on. Kathleen was five now and Pete was four. In the mornings Kathleen would wake up when the roosters began to crow. She would run into the kitchen and sit on a stool while Mary finished making breakfast.

"Oh, Grandma, I love the smell of frying bacon."

Mary said, "When you have cooked bacon for as many years as I have, you don't notice the smell." While she spoke, she removed a dish towel from the top of a bowl containing bread dough. "This hasn't raised near enough." She replaced the towel.

Just then Evan and Dub walked into the kitchen. They had finished milking the cows and separating the cream from the milk. At the same time Pete, still rubbing his eyes, walked into the kitchen.

Mary said, "Looks like everyone is ready for breakfast. Kathleen, would you set the table for us?"

"Could I, Grandma?"

"You certainly may. Folks it will be another 15 minutes before it is ready. I need to fry the eggs and we'll just have toast this morning."

Evan helped himself to a cup of coffee and went out on the porch. Dub got coffee also, and then followed Evan out to the porch. Pete decided he would join the men so he walked out to the porch and sat next to Evan.

Kathleen and Pete went home the first Friday in July. They didn't know at the time that it would be their last visit for five years.

Pictures taken on their 25th Wedding Anniversary

CHAPTER 15

Wisdom is better than weapons of war

The government started a peacetime draft. All males between the ages of 18 and 35 had to register and could be drafted. Dub was on his way into town to register when Evan said, "I'm going with you. We need to try to get you excused from this draft. I need you here to help run this place."

"Dad, I'm willing to go if it is necessary."

"I'm sure you are, Dub, but we are not in a war and you will do more good here than you would in the army even if there is a war. People will need food and meat. Somebody has to be available to produce those things. That somebody is farmers and ranchers. Dub, I can't work all day. If we are going to do our part then you must be here to do it."

An appeal was made for Dub to be classified as necessary at home for farming purposes. The fact that Evan had a heart attack nine years ago influenced the draft board to classify Dub as necessary farm labor. The board did tell Dub that the classification could change.

Sunday morning, December 7, 1941, began cold but with bright sunshine. Evan suggested, "Babe, we've not been to church for a while, let's go this morning."

"You're right, we haven't been for a while. We really should go more often," Mary responded.

"Do you want to go with us, Dub?"

"Think I'll just stay here."

After they returned home Mary said, "Looks like Dub has gotten himself something to eat. It will be awhile before I have dinner ready for us." Mary put on her apron.

"Take your time; I'm not hungry at the moment." Evan got out the cards and started playing solitaire. It was 2 o'clock when they finished their meal. Mary cleared the table and Evan went back to his card game. It was a lazy afternoon.

Around 4 o'clock the phone rang. Mary answered, "It's Bob Shelby. He asked if we had our radio on. When I said no, he said to turn the radio on. We have been attacked by the Japanese!"

"What?" Evan quickly turned the radio on. There was an excited announcer telling about Pearl Harbor being bombed. The news was on every station. Announcers told about ships destroyed and men killed. It was as if Armageddon had occurred. The Furmans were stunned the same as all other Americans. The United States had never been challenged like this before. After listening for quite awhile Evan said, "I thought we would be attacked by Germany. I never thought about Japan attacking us."

They continued listening; they could not believe what they were hearing. The news reporter told of two waves of planes sweeping over the Hawaiian Islands beginning at 10:48 a.m. Hawaiian time. Four battleships, three cruisers, and other types of ships were sunk and badly damaged. They were not sure of the death toll. It was thought to be in the hundreds.

The phone rang again. This time it was Milla. A short time later, Jessie called. Then Ruth called. All over the United States, phone lines became so busy that operators could not handle all the calls. Connections were not made and others were broken off. America would never be the same.

The next morning Evan drove to town just to buy a newspaper. The headline covered a third of the front page. It read **WAR.** The President was to speak at 12:30 to a joint session of congress. It would be broadcasted on the radio.

Evan purchased another battery for the radio and hurried home. At 12:30 he turned the radio on and anxiously awaited the news.

The President began speaking, "Yesterday, December 7, 1941, a date which will live in infamy, the United States was suddenly and deliberately attacked by naval and air forces of the Empire of Japan." He asked congress to declare war on Japan, which they did. Soon afterward war was also declared on Germany and Italy. America would have to fight on two different fronts. The nation had never done that before. It would be an overwhelming task.

There was a feeling of unity throughout the nation. The war united everyone behind the President. People were no longer Democrats or Republicans; they were Americans. All across America, recruiting stations were jammed with volunteers and had to go on 24 hour duty to sign up recruits. Dub and Evan had another conversation about serving in the Army or helping with all the work that needed to be done on their place.

"Dad, I feel like I should sign up for military service. A lot of the guys I know are going."

"Dub, I know you want to help. Remember what I told you before; you will be more helpful by staying here. I can't do everything that needs done anymore. We need to fulfill our part by providing beef and wheat. The army will need to be fed. Like I told you before, there will be a great need for beef and farm produce. With so many men leaving farms and going into the service, there will be a shortage of farm workers. Who's going to fill that need?"

"I never thought about that. If I get drafted, what will happen then?"

"Let's hope it does not come to that but if it does, we will just have to cope with it."

For the next several months the war news was not favorable. In the Pacific Ocean area, Japan had the upper hand. Japan attacked the Philippine Islands and the American army was retreating; they surrendered early in 1942. In Europe, the German Army faced only local underground forces, since British and French armies had been pushed off the continent two years earlier.

Jessie sent a letter informing Evan and Mary that Chick had been called to active duty. He would be in the Navy with the rank of Chief Petty Officer. She was going to follow him as long as possible.

Evan said, "I'm not surprised. I just hope Chick will not be put in danger."

Mary replied, "It's a good thing they don't have any children yet since Jessie is going to follow him who knows where and for how long. That wouldn't be a good life for a little one."

"Chick could be assigned to a ship. That's what happened to my brother in the First World War. If that happens, Jessie may come here to live."

"That would be fine. Then we would know Jessie was safe. I think about what might happen to Milla and her kids if Larry goes into the military. Do you think he might be drafted?"

"I can't say for sure, but since he has two kids and is now the fire chief in Rushville, I doubt if he will."

"Evan, how long do you think this war will last?"

"It's hard to say. I'm afraid it will be a long time."

War changed daily living. Rationing became a new way of life. Everything from sugar and meat to shoes and automobile tires were in short supply. Books with stamps were issued to all families. They were used to purchase rationed commodities, which was most things. Everyone changed their living patterns to fit the astringent supply of commodities.

Mary said, "Evan, you won't be getting as many cinnamon rolls and pies like you have been getting. Sugar has been limited so much that anything I bake will be a treat."

"Babe, that's a small sacrifice on our part. We will have plenty of other food. What I'm concerned about getting enough gas to stack hay and combine wheat. I read that farmers will get an exemption on gas rationing. I hope that is not some political talk." This was not political talk; in fact, Democrats and Republicans worked together like never before.

Then Mary asked, "If all this helps to shorten the war, I don't mind in the least. Do you?"

"I agree. The ironic thing in all this is for ten years we didn't have the money to buy clothes or much of anything. Now we have more money, but we still are limited in what we can buy because of rationing."

Evan's comment about gasoline registered with Mary. "Evan, with gasoline being rationed, how can you plant or harvest anything? Milla said that Larry got a B sticker for their car, which allowed them to buy eight gallons of gas a week."

"Remember last week when I said farmers would get a gas exemption; it happened. Farmers and ranchers are being issued a non-highway ration allowance that will provide additional gas. We can't waste any gas, but we should be able to work our land."

Evan and Mary received two important news letters that year.

The first was from Jessie; Chick was assigned to the naval base at Norfolk, Virginia. He would be a training instructor for incoming recruits. They thought he would stay there for the duration of the war.

"Oh Evan, this is good news. Jessie's husband is going to stay in the United States."

"Yes it is. I just hope he will remain there and not be reassigned."

The second letter came from Jim, indicating he had remarried and a month later was drafted. He was to report for duty in the Army, and take basic training in Missouri. That was all he knew.

"I'm not surprised that Jim remarried since he didn't come home after his divorce to Helen. I thought he might. Wonder what his new wife is like?"

Mary answered, "He says her name is Frances Bruin. He doesn't have much else to say about her. I don't know why. Being drafted is a terrible way to start a marriage."

"Yes, it is. I hoped since he had two kids, he might be spared. Maybe he was drafted because he and his new wife don't have any kids."

"Evan, I feel so bad about what is going on in the world. I've read about boys we know who have been killed and I worry about Jim and Chick. Will Dub be the next one to go?"

"I don't think Dub will be drafted; at least, not for a while. I hope not. Everyone worries about family men in the war. I see little flags in many front windows of homes, some with two or three stars, and my heart aches for those families."

"I know what you mean. The mothers and wives of service men worry about their return. I thank God that we have been spared from having one of ours in a dangerous place. I guess everyone is facing this one day at a time."

"That's all we can do, Babe. If only we could read some good news, it would help. The war goes on and on with very little positive being said."

Morale boosting news did fill the newspapers and the radio reports in late April 1942. The accounts told of General Jimmy Doolittle leading a flight of 16 B-25's on a raid to bomb Tokyo, Japan. The planes were launched from the aircraft carrier Hornet, and successfully bombed Tokyo. Although all planes were lost, most of the crews did survive.

Evan said to Dub, "Good for our boys! They took it right to the Japs. Now the Japanese know they are vulnerable. Now there has been some payback for Pearl Harbor."

"So do you think the fighting will stop now?"

"Oh no, the war will still go on. I would think that the Japanese people might be more skeptical about everything their leaders tell them about how safe and superior they are."

That spring, Churchill convinced Roosevelt that there should be a joint attack on the Germans in Africa. Roosevelt agreed and selected General Dwight Eisenhower to be the Commanding General of American Forces, European Theater. Shortly thereafter, the British proposed General Montgomery to be selected as Supreme Allied Commander of all forces. But after much political debate, they finally agreed to Eisenhower in that position.

When June rolled around that year, it was obvious that Milla's two kids would not be coming for a visit. Evan said to Mary, "As much as I would like to see Kathleen and Pete, I don't think it's possible."

Mary responded, "No, it isn't. The trains don't have any empty seats because of all the soldiers being moved from one place to another. And with the gas rationed, we can't go get them."

"Speaking of the rationing reminded me that we are due for a new ration book this month. I'll pick it up next time we're in town."

"Oh, good! We can buy some sugar then."

After reading the newspaper one morning, Evan said, "I see Tom Becker is having an auction Saturday. He joined the Army Air Corp so he is selling out. I think I'll go. Does anyone want to go with me?"

Dub said, "I'd like to go. Maybe I could buy some calves cheap."

"You might; but they may sell all his calves in one lot. It would take several dollars to buy them all. What I'm interested in is the John Deere tractor he owns."

Evan and Dub got to the sale early Saturday. "Dub, there's not as many men here as I thought there would be. I guess most have found what they need at some of the other auctions that have been going on. Either that or there just isn't that many men farming now."

"So do you think the small crowd will mean lower bids?"

"It could, just depends on how bad someone wants something. I want to look over Tom's tractor. I'm going to bid on it if the price doesn't get too high."

Dub said, "I going to look over the calves."

Dub was outbid on the calves. He was unable to go very high. Evan was successful in obtaining the tractor. "I had to pay more than I planned, but we needed a tractor and there sure are not any new ones available. This one should be fine for our needs. It's only four years old."

"How are you going to get it home?"

"Well, part of the deal was a free delivery within 40 miles. It was 38 miles over here, so that puts us just under the wire."

Dub asked Evan, "Since they're going to deliver it, would you mind riding home with whoever delivers the tractor?"

"I suppose I could, if they will load it up and leave when the auction is over. Why do you ask?"

"There is a gal in Merriman I would like to go see. I need the pickup to go there."

"Who's the girl?"

"Iva Grieser; I've had a couple of dates with her. With gas being rationed I don't get to see her very often."

"Since we are this close to Merriman, you take the pickup and go see her. I'll get home one way or another."

Dub made a lot of phone calls to Merriman, but face to face contact with Iva was severely limited. What few times they had been together, they had found many common interests. Dub liked being with Iva; he just found it difficult to do so. Finally Dub had enough; he asked Iva to marry him and she accepted. They were married in early November in her parents' home.

Before 1942 ended, the tide of the war began to turn. Evan was glued to the radio. Day after day he heard reports on the war effort.

Bombing raids were destroying German factories and damaging German Army supply lines in Europe. In December, Americans landed in Northern Africa. At last, Americans were fighting the German Army on the ground.

In the Pacific theater, the Battle of Midway was fought in June.

The U.S. Navy decisively defeated the Japanese Navy. The Japanese lost four aircraft carriers and one heavy cruiser. After this success, the Americans went on the offensive. The marines attacked the Solomon Islands. Victory was achieved at Guadalcanal in February, 1943. The United States slowly gained naval and air supremacy in the Pacific and began capturing islands one at a time.

On the European front, the Germans and Italians had been defeated in Africa. In July, the Allies invaded Sicily and began the assault on Italy. The fighting in Italy continued throughout all of 1943. Mussolini was deposed and the Italian government fell. Hitler's armies filled the void quickly by taking control of Rome.

In other parts of Europe, Allied planes were bombing German factories around the clock. England became a staging ground for the invasion of Europe. American troops and materials were everywhere on the island.

In August of 1943 Evan and Mary received a letter from Jessie.

Dear Folks,

We are a little closer to you now. Chick has been transferred to the Great Lakes Naval Station. I have found a place to live in Lake Forest which is really a suburb of Chicago. Chick gets liberty every other weekend and a free night once in awhile.

The other big news I have to tell you is that I am going to have a baby in mid September. I am getting along fine but I will be glad when he or she finally arrives. We will try to call you after the baby is born.

Love,
Jessie

Chick called on September 17th, Jessie delivered a healthy 5lb. 3oz. girl. They named her Susan Judith. Evan answered the phone and congratulated Chick. He hung up and told Mary, "Babe we are Grandparents again."

"Jessie had her baby; boy or girl?"

"It was a girl named Susan Judith. She weighted 5lb. 3oz. Baby and mother are doing fine."

Six weeks later, Dub and Iva brought another granddaughter into the world. Her name was Diana Lee. Evan said to Mary, "We now have six grandchildren. Do you think we will have anymore?"

"I wouldn't be surprised, but only time will tell."

Family life took a backseat to the war effort. Evan continued to listen to the news reports on the radio every day. He would tell Mary, "Most of the war news seems to be about what is happening in the Pacific. The lives being lost there makes me sad. War is a terrible thing. I would guess the invasion of Europe can't be far away and then the deaths will be even greater."

In the spring of 1944 a letter came from Milla telling that both Kathleen and Pete were sick. The doctor told them it was strep throat but it never went away. Now he says its rheumatic fever. There's not much he can do. He said they must remain in bed for several weeks and give them aspirin if the fever gets too high. He wants to try to get some new kind of medicine; however, with the war needs taking most of the supply, he's not sure he can.

Evan took the news hard. "Lord, how I pray they will be alright."

"Evan, those two are strong and Milla will take good care of them. They will be fine. You just wait and see."

"I think I'll call Milla and ask if we should try to go over to see them. Or is there anything we could do? I don't care if gas is being rationed."

"Evan, I don't think we can do anything. Milla will be grateful knowing you are concerned."

"With my grandkids sick and needing medicine they can't get, I would fight the whole world to get it for them. Oh how I wish this war would end tomorrow. Then getting this medicine would not be a problem. Sometimes I wonder; does this war have any end in sight?"

June brought a big change in the war in Europe. The long awaited invasion began. This was good but the reports brought more depressing news about the loss of lives in the war. The front page of the newspaper read:

On June the 6th of 1944 the Allies began the largest amphibious invasion in history. 5,000 ships carried men and supplies or supported the invasion in one manner or another. 160,000 Allied troops went ashore on the French coast in five different locations and 24,000 paratroopers were dropped behind the coastal defenses. The loss in American lives was staggering.

Evan felt this was a big step toward the end of the war. The over whelming cost of lives made Evan wonder how many of those killed might he know. Every evening Evan listened to Lowell Thomas reporting the war news. He told how the fighting in France was intense. Evan heard how slowly the Allied armies gained ground. But by the end of August, all of northern France had been liberated. Two weeks later, most of the remainder of France was under control of the Allied armies. Still the war in Europe continued through the winter.

In the Pacific, the Philippine Islands were liberated in late 1944. One morning, Evan put down the newspaper and said, "Babe, it's only a matter of time before this war is over. Unfortunately, I'm afraid there will be many more American solders die before it ends."

The newspapers reported the attack on two islands in 1945. Iwo Jima and Okinawa became familiar names. The loss of American lives was high for the victory that moved American forces closer to Japan.

In Europe, Allied armies crossed the Rhine River in March, 1945.

Then on the morning of May 8, 1945, the news reported -

GERMANY SURRENDERS

"Does this mean the war is over?" Dub asked.

Evan answered, "It is in Europe, but not in the Pacific. I would guess plans are being made right now to attack Japan. I can't imagine how difficult that will be. With their suicide mentality, it will cost many American lives."

President Truman must have felt the same way because he authorized the dropping of an atomic bomb on the Japanese city of Hiroshima. Then three days later, another atomic bomb was dropped on Nagasaki. Japan had no will to fight any longer.

On August 14, 1945, they agreed to surrender. It became official aboard the Battleship Missouri on September 2, 1945. "Now, Dub, it is finally over. Praise the Lord!"

CHAPTER 16

Generations come and generations go,
but the earth remains forever

There was peace and hope in everyone's mind. It had been a long war. Men came home to resume their civilian lives. American society was about to change. For more than four years people could not buy many things. Now the rationing era was over and people had money in their pockets. There was a pent up desire to buy. Worn out appliances, cars and tires needed to be replaced. Factories changed from producing war equipment to civilian commodities. Appliances, radios and automobiles soon became available. New clothing and shoes began to appear and were quickly sold. Slowly prosperity began to take charge.

Both Jim and Chick were released from military service. Jim went back to Indianapolis and returned to his job at the dairy. Chick and Jessie moved to Cheyenne where Jessie taught school again and Chick became a stock broker.

As 1945 came to an end, two days before Christmas, Iva gave birth to their second child, Bryon Thomas. Mary said to Evan, "Now we have four grandsons and three granddaughters. How do you feel about that?"

"You know how much I like kids, but I have to confess having seven grandchildren makes me feel older. It doesn't seem that long ago that I had four little ones around me and didn't know what to do. Looking back I must admit that was two World Wars and a long depression ago. Guess that does make it a long time back."

Mary smiled, "Someone said, time waits for no man."

"True, time moves on. Over those years we have seen a lot of changes. Remember the first automobiles and how you had to carry spare tires whenever you traveled very far?"

Mary answered, "Didn't you have to change a tire the first time we drove from Hay Springs to Gordon? If I remember correctly, you got upset because the tire blew out."

"I don't remember that part." Evan wanted to change the subject. He said, "I think distances are something else that has changed. When you and I married, I never would have believed that someday our kids would be spread over half of the United States. Seems like since the war ended, people move around a lot more. Why, nowadays no one thinks a thing about driving 50 or 100 miles."

"Evan, before you analyze the world, let's be grateful that Dub lives right here by us and Milla's family only live 2 hours away. And Pete spends most of the summer with us and Kathleen comes over for a few days at a time."

"I am grateful for that. I just wish we could see Jessie's family and Jim and his boys like we do the others."

That first summer Milla's kids came to visit, Evan said to Mary, "The kids seem fine. When they got sick I was afraid they might have some permanent handicap."

"Yes, they both seem fine and full of life. We may have our hands full."

"Well, if we do, it will be a good thing. I'm so glad they are here. I missed their visits for the last five years."

Pete idolized his Grandpa. Where ever Evan went, Pete was his shadow. One summer day Evan was sitting on the step to the tool shed sharpening sickle blades for the mower. Pete looked toward the house and yelled, "Grandpa there is smoke coming out of the bedroom window!"

Evan never looked up and kept on sharpening sickle blades. He said in calm voice, "Maybe you should go see what is happening."

Pete ran to the house, burst in the door and ran to the bedroom yelling, "Grandma, the house is on fire!" Mary met him at the bedroom door and backed out so he could not see inside. "Everything is alright Pete. The vacuum cleaner just over heated." But Pete did get a glance inside the bedroom and saw a cigarette in an ash tray. Mary kept working Pete away from the bedroom. "You can go on back to Grandpa and tell him everything is ok."

When Pete got back to Evan, he never stopped working, he just ask, "Everything alright at the house?"

"Grandma said the vacuum cleaner overheated."

"That's so." Pete never noticed the smirk on his Grandpa's face. Later that night Mary expressed her anger at Evan for the trick he had pulled.

Pete was confused and wondered what was going on. The next day he asked Iva, "Does Grandma smoke?"

"What makes you think your Grandma smokes?" Pete told her what had happened yesterday. Iva laughed and said, "Well now you know what the rest of the family knows. Yes, your Grandma does smoke but she does not want anyone to know about it."

"But you all do, so why does she want to keep it secret?"

"Your Grandma is a little ashamed of her habit. She feels smoking is not lady like. So we do not discuss it or let on that we know she smokes. Pete, your Grandpa was just pulling a joke on you. I'll bet Grandma jumped all over him last night."

The following winter was cold with heavy snow falls. One January morning when Mary looked out the window she said, "The weatherman certainly missed it this time. He said we would just get snow flurries and the snow must be seven or eight inches deep out there."

Evan said, "He didn't miss it. We got flurries – seven inches of flurries."

"Dub is coming this way with a shovel; he will clear your seven inches of flurries away from the front door."

After Dub finished clearing a path away from the house, he went inside and asked, "Do you want me to check on the cattle?"

Evan said, "They should be alright if they can get to enough hay. You might check on that this afternoon."

Shortly after the spring weather began to warm, Evan said, "Let's call Milla and see if her kids can come again this summer to visit when school ends. Kathleen and Pete rode the train to Merriman where Evan met them at the station.

After giving them a big hug Evan said, "You two sure have grown. What has your mother been feeding the two of you?"

Kathleen looked at him with tears in her eyes, "We didn't think you would want us to come any more since Dianna and Bryon are living next door now."

"That idea is nonsense; you both were here just last summer. Whatever gave you that idea?"

Kathleen answered, "We never heard from you all winter. We thought you had forgotten us."

"Steer calf I could never forget the two of you. I missed you more than you will ever know. No more of that kind of talk. Let's go home."

Kathleen squinted up her eyes and said, "Don't call me a steer calf. I am not a boy!"

As they got into the truck Pete said, "Look Grandpa, I brought my toy tractor with me. I paid ten cents of my own money for it."

"Even though it's not green, that's a fine looking tractor."

"I know. They didn't have any green ones."

"Well, there are other tractors besides John Deere."

Evan patted Kathleen on the leg and asked, "Well little gal, what did you bring?"

"I didn't bring anything. I'm going to help Grandma with the strawberries and the green beans."

Pete chimed in, "I want to help too."

The dust flew as they drove across the Nebraska and South Dakota state line.

The next morning Kathleen asked, "Can we go to the creek?"

Mary said, "I don't think that is a very good idea." So they went to Evan and asked the same question.

Evan thought for a minute then said, "Alright, but don't fall in. That creek has only two feet of water, but six feet of mud."

"We'll be careful, Grandpa."

As they threw some rocks into the water, Pete asked, "Do you really think there is six feet of mud in the creek?"

"No, I think Grandpa just said that to keep us out of the water."

Pete started removing his shoes, "Let's find out." He stepped into the edge of the water and sunk in a couple of inches. "It feels funny with mud coming up between my toes. It's not six feet deep."

Kathleen removed her shoes and joined him. They walked up and down the edge testing the deepness of the mud. Laughing and daring one another to go out into deeper water. When they got tired of the mud walking, they picked up their shoes and returned to the house.

Mary was picking strawberries. She took one look at the two and said, "Where have you been? You both have mud up to your knees and your clothes are filthy! Go to the water hose and wash yourselves off before you go into the house. Then you're both going to take a bath."

Evan walked upon the scene hiding his grin. "Now, Babe, they haven't hurt anything, so don't be hard on them."

"You're the one I should be hard on because you told them they could go to the creek."

Evan whispered to Kathleen, "I guess we all are in trouble."

After supper was over that evening, Mary and Kathleen cleared the dishes from the table. As Evan got up, he said to Pete, "We Swedes need to stay out of the way while the bull hunks wash the dishes."

Pete chuckled but Kathleen said to Mary, "Grandma, I don't like being called a bull hunk!"

"Grandpa is just teasing you. He loves you and wouldn't say anything to make you feel bad. Just ignore him went he calls you that."

"Is he really a Swede?"

"Not that I know. Just like us, he's an American."

The summer was hot. Evan always wore a wide brimmed straw hat. He would say, "It's the only shade I have when we put up hay."

He and Dub managed to stack hay without any other help. Evan would pull the mower with the tractor and Dub guided two horses pulling the hay rake. After the grass had been cut and raked into rows, it needed to be stacked into piles.

While the two were attaching a lift fork to the tractor Evan said, "As soon as new equipment becomes available, we are going to replace what we have been using."

Dub asked, "What are you going to buy?"

"I want to get a Jay Hawk stacker, for one thing. It will do a better job than this fork, and it is more maneuverable."

"The way you talk, you have more than that in mind."

"I do. A Model A John Deere would be great and I have been thinking about buying a combine."

"Where are you going to get the money for all that?"

"I Think I have enough for about everything. During the war we couldn't buy anything, so we bought war bonds or just banked what we earned. Now the money is available. If the price isn't too high I can buy the equipment we need."

The Jay Hawk was the first to be available, then Evan bought a new John Deere a month later.

In the fall, Evan had a good yield of wheat which allowed him to purchase a wind charger that generated electricity. Storage batteries were placed in the storm cellar and wires connected to both houses. "Babe, we are just like the town folks. We have lights, an inside bathroom, and a phone. What more could a person want?"

"I think the best part is we won't be dependent upon the ice man. The electric refrigerator is wonderful. I don't worry about food spoiling any more."

"I never knew you worried about food spoiling."

"I did when the ice melted and it wasn't time for him to come around or we were not going to town."

Crop yields stayed good and the price for beef remained high. In the spring of 1947 Evan bought a new Chevrolet. "Babe, we've got a new car; let's drive to Indiana and visit Jim and the boys. We could go after we finish branding the new calves."

"I think that's a good idea. It's been a long time since we last saw them. I'll write a letter to Jim and let him know we are coming. Maybe he can take a few days off from work."

When the branding was finished and the wheat had been planted, they packed for the three day trip to Indiana. The morning they left Mary said, "It looks like it is going to be a good day."

As they drove through Martin, Evan replied, "All days are good; some are just better than others."

"Evan are you an Irishman? You are so full of blarney."

"You're asking me that after all these years? I'm not sure where my ancestors came from. Anyway I agree with you. It is a good day and this is going to be a good trip."

The trip went well until Evan missed a turn in Illinois and made a U-turn. Almost immediately he was stopped by a policeman. The policeman walked up to the driver's door and said, "Mister, please show me your drivers' license and car registration."

Evan reached into the glove box and pulled out the registration form. Handing it to the policeman, he said "We live in South Dakota and a driver's license is not required."

The policeman gave Evan a surprised look. He was having difficulty accepting that answer. Evan could see he was not being believed. He said, "It is true. South Dakota maybe the only state in the union that does not require a driver's license but it is true."

For a while it looked like there was going to be trouble for Evan and Mary. After a little more conversation, the policeman said, "Mister, you and your wife look like honest people so I'll believe what you are telling me. But I sure am going to check this out when I get back to the station."

"Thank you, officer. You will find it is true."

After they arrived at Jim's house there was a lot of reminiscing. Jim introduced his wife, Frances. Then he said, "Tomorrow I'll show you the 500 mile race track. It is two and a half miles around the track."

Evan was impressed with the 500 mile race track. "I've heard about this race track. I never thought it was this big. Seeing it is something else. Watching a race take place must be quite an experience. Have you been here to see a race?"

"No, but I have delivered milk to the race track; tradition dictates that the winner drink milk. For the last three years the company I work for has supplied the bottle of milk that the driver drinks."

"The winner drinks milk? That's hard to believe."

"It's true. Right after the winner is congratulated and given the trophy, he takes a big drink of milk from a bottle."

"I'm surprised. I would have guessed he would drink champagne."

They drove around Indianapolis looking at the few things there were to see, and the place were Jim worked.

Evan and Mary wanted to see Jim's boys, so he arranged for Mike and Bill to come for a day while their grandparents were staying with him. The first thing Bill asked Evan, "What do you think of Indiana land, Grandpa?"

Evan replied, "I don't know."

Bill was surprised with that answer. "What do you mean?"

"I can't see very much, all the trees are in the way."

"Gee, I never thought of it that way."

"It's all about where you're living. People always think where they live is the best place on earth. I guess that makes for a lot of great places. But for me, I like the openness of the prairie country. There one can see for miles if he is on a high hill."

Mike asked, "Is Shep still alive?"

"No, he died three years ago."

"What about Old Blue? I remember riding him every time we were at your place."

"I'm afraid he's gone too. But we still have horses at our place."

That night, Evan and Mary drove the boys back to their mother's apartment. As they returned to Jim's house Evan said, "It's sad the boys don't have a father and mother in the same house. But it hasn't affected them from what I can see."

"They are good boys, even if they are Furmans."

"Well, since they are Furmans, I wouldn't expect anything else."

Two days later, as Evan and Mary returned to South Dakota, Evan said, "It was good to hear both Jim and Helen say the boys could come out to visit us next summer. I sure hope that works out."

"This summer is not over. Milla's two are supposed to come for a visit next week. Then let's call Jessie and see if Susan could come for a visit before her school starts this fall."

"That's a good idea Babe. We haven't seen her for a while." The conversation stopped while Evan drove through Springfield, Illinois. Evan concentrated on the traffic and Mary thought about what she needed to do when they got back home.

A few miles later Evan said, "I have been on this earth 60 years and I think both of us have had a good life. Sure, there were some struggles but we never had any trouble from any of our kids. Now they have children of their own. And they are living their lives the best they can I guess. I just wish there were some things that were different."

"You're thinking about Jim and Helen, aren't you?"

"Yes. I always liked Helen. I'm sorry they're not still married. But I was thinking about our other kids too."

"Evan, you can't live their lives for them."

"I know that. Like all parents, I want a good, trouble-free life for my children. I do thank the Lord that they all have money in their pockets and a roof over their heads. There was a time or two when I wondered if we would."

"Should I say Amen?"

"If you want -- Now let's all turn to page 148 in our hymnals."

"Evan!!! You are hopeless."

"What? Don't you think I could be a preacher?"

"Heavens, no! You don't go to church enough to know what happens inside of one."

"Maybe not, but I know there is a God and who he is, that should count for something."

"I never heard you talk like this."

"I never felt the need to, but I always believed in God. I remember my Pa telling me about God creating the world and I never doubted what he said."

"I have been married to you for almost 32 years. I am just now seeing a side to you that I didn't know existed."

"Well, tune in next week and see what wonders happen to this prairie family. And now, a word from our sponsor."

"Evan, you will never be a radio announcer. I don't think you will ever change."

The next day they crossed the Missouri River. Evan said, "A few more miles and the view will open up. That's when I feel like I'm in God's country. Right after we get home, the first thing I am going to do is walk out in the west pasture just to get the city stink blown off me."

"Shame on you! You make city living sound undesirable. But it will be good to get back home. I'll bake you a pie the first chance I get."

"Being in God's country and having pie; what more could a man want?"

EPILOGUE

Evan and Mary moved from their place east of Martin, South Dakota to Chadron, Nebraska in 1961. There were two reasons for the move.

The first reason was Evan's health. He knew his time on earth was growing short and he did not want to leave Mary living five miles from a town. The second reason was their granddaughter, Diana, wanted to go college. There was a college in Chadron where she could attend and continue living with them. This would make her education more affordable.

After they had moved, Evan was asked about living in town. He answered, "It's alright for old folks and I have to admit I am one now. Guess I'll manage until the butter Babe made runs out. Don't know what I'll do then."

The butter Mary had made just before they moved, lasted 18 months. Evan tolerated 'store-bought' butter for another 18 months. He died March 4, 1964. He was buried in the Rushville cemetery where his father and mother were buried.

Evan had lived in two different centuries. He was born on the open prairie. He died in a small city. He had known both wealth and meager means. He lived believing a person should be honest and hard working. He was respected by many people and admired by his grandchildren. He was not a great man or well-known. He was a good man that set an example for future generations.

Picture taken of Evan, Mary and children in mid-1950's

Milla Jim Mary Ruth Jessie Evan
Dub

The Grandchildren

Susan Mike Tom Diana

Kathleen Lawrence

Bill

CHAPTER CAPTIONS

Chapter 1:	God is in heaven and you are on the earth.	Ecclesiastes 5:2
Chapter 2:	I saw that wisdom is better than folly.	Ecclesiastes 2:13
Chapter 3:	If two lie down together, they will keep warm.	Ecclesiastes 4:11
Chapter 4:	Death is the destiny of every man.	Ecclesiastes 7:2
Chapter 5:	The end of a matter is better than its beginning.	Ecclesiastes 7:8
Chapter 6:	A good name is better than a fine perfume.	Ecclesiastes 7:1
Chapter 7:	Do not pay attention to every word people say.	Ecclesiastes 7:21
Chapter 8:	When times are good be happy: but when times are bad, consider; God made one as well as the other.	Ecclesiastes7:14
Chapter 9:	Do not say, "Why were the old days better then these."	Ecclesiastes 7:10
Chapter 10:	There is a proper time and procedure for every matter.	Ecclesiastes 8:6
Chapter 11:	Words from a wise man's mouth are gracious.	Ecclesiastes 10:12
Chapter 12:	No man has power over the wind to contain it.	Ecclesiastes 8:8
Chapter 13:	Whatever your hand finds to do, do it with all your might.	Ecclesiastes 9:10
Chapter 14:	Since no man knows the future, who can tell him what is to come.	Ecclesiastes 8:7
Chapter 15:	Wisdom is better than weapons of war.	Ecclesiastes 9:18
Chapter 16:	Generations come and generations go, but the earth remains.	Ecclesiastes 1:4

www.ingramcontent.com/pod-product-compliance
Ingram Content Group UK Ltd.
Pitfield, Milton Keynes, MK11 3LW, UK
UKHW041945190726
13854UKWH00004B/1799